Pressing FORWARD

Faith, Culture, and
African American Youth

Carmichael Crutchfield with Denise Janssen
Foreword by Reginald Blount

JUDSON PRESS
PUBLISHERS SINCE 1824
VALLEY FORGE, PA

Pressing Forward
Faith, Culture, and African American Youth

Judson Press has made every effort to trace the ownership of all quotes. In the event of a question arising from the use of a quote, we regret any error made and will be pleased to make the necessary correction in future printings and editions of this book.

Bible quotations in this volume are from the New Revised Standard Version of the Bible, copyright © 1989 by the Division of Christian Education of the National Council of the Churches of Christ in the United States of America. Used by permission. All rights reserved.

Interior and cover design by Wendy Ronga, Hampton Design Group.

Library of Congress Cataloging-in-Publication data
Names: Crutchfield, Carmichael, author. | Janssen, Denise, author. Title: Pressing forward: faith, culture, and African American youth / Carmichael Crutchfield with Denise Janssen. Description: Valley Forge, PA: Judson Press, 2022. | Includes bibliographical references. Identifiers: LCCN 2021038078 (print) | LCCN 2021038079 (ebook) | ISBN 9780817018344 (paperback) | ISBN 9780817082383 (epub) Subjects: LCSH: Church work with African American youth. | Spiritual formation—Christianity. Classification: LCC BV4468.2.A34 C78 2022 (print) | LCC BV4468.2.A34 (ebook) | DDC 259/.2308996073—dc23
LC record available at https://lccn.loc.gov/2021038078
LC ebook record available at https://lccn.loc.gov/2021038079

Printed in the U.S.A.
First printing, 2022.

Contents

Foreword

There was a time when the Black Church was instrumental in meeting many needs within the African American community, primarily through the Church's role as educator and nurturer. The Black Church served as the socializing agent of self-worth, hope-building, and promising purpose. There was a time when the Black Church reminded persons of African descent that they were somebody, even if the dominant society worked hard to convince otherwise. When African Americans were denied various opportunities and were the object of blatant disrespect, oppression and abuse (both physically and emotionally), there was a time when the Black Church provided not only moral and intellectual instruction, but also through such instruction, offered and instilled a sense of self-worth and self-determination in youth as well as adults. There was a time when the Black Church succeeded in helping many to realize that despite blatant attacks against their personhood, they were still children of God.

Our current times seem to provide somewhat similar, yet also unique challenges to the African American community, particularly in the faith formation of its youth, as the community struggles with a crippling sense of nihilism. It's what Cornel West once described as "a life of horrifying meaninglessness, hopelessness, and [most important] lovelessness,"[1] and what Ellis Cose coined "the rage of a privileged class"—the immense disenchantment of middle class African Americans who've played by the rules and embraced the

American Dream, only to experience a "broken covenant."[2] The Black Church also finds itself struggling with its own understanding of its identity and purpose. Once the center of the African American community, the Black Church now finds itself on the periphery of African American life and culture, at least within the last generation or two. The peripheral placement is partly due to a rising number of unchurched in the African American community, which breeds a loss of communal memory. The unchurched are not intimately familiar with the role the Black Church played in the past in shaping faith and personhood. Those who are unchurched now turn to other sources for moral instruction, spiritual enlightenment, and hope-building, or to no sources at all.

The Black Church's peripheral placement is also because of its struggle to be relevant to more effectively "serve the present age." One obvious example is the absence of the traditional Black Church being an agent of self-worth, hope-building, and promising purpose for the young people leading the Black Lives Matter Movement or the demonstrations and demands for justice following the murders of George Floyd, Breonna Taylor, Ahmaud Arbery, and others. There are still attacks on the personhood of African American youth today. W. E. B. Du Bois' double consciousness is still warring in the spirits of African American youth, as they struggle to discover who they are and their reason for being. Yet the Black Church has either lost its ability or abdicated its responsibility to offer a counter-message to today's youth in search of faith, hope, love, meaning, and purpose. What hope is being offered to African American youth who are trying to navigate the stormy seas of adolescence to adulthood?

While it is clear there are some external challenges that African American youth encounter that obviously still exist—such as racism, classism, sexism, and homophobism, as well as new challenges emerging from technology, globalization, and consumerism—Dr. Carmichael Crutchfield and Dr. Denise Janssen highlight that there are internal, spiritual challenges African American youth wrestle with as well. There are pastoral concerns that the Black Church must take seriously if it is to be relevant to twenty-first-century young people. These are commitments that must be instilled in the socialization, in the faith formation taking place in today's Black churches. In the Black Church, youth ministry must include more than "traditional church" indoctrination. Our young people need more than programs! They need congregations willing to pastor, willing to shepherd, nurture, and guide them through those challenging seas from adolescence to adulthood. The Black Church must reclaim her significant and vital role in the faith formation of Black youth. The Black Church must commit herself to be relevant again to a generation desperately needing the "gospel," a good news that counters some of the destructive messages offered by today's popular culture. The Black Church must commit herself again to aiding Black youth to discover their personhood in the Imago Dei, the image of God, versus the personhood that the dominant culture chooses to craft for them. I still believe it is the institution that can best aid African American young people to better understand who they are in the eyes of God through Jesus Christ and help them discover God's purpose for their lives.

It is why I am so grateful to Crutchfield and Janssen for offering this passionate pastoral and educational resource that gives voice to the needs and yearnings they heard echoing from the hearts of African American young people. This book is a clarion call to the Black Church, the institution that has been vital to the lives of Black people for centuries, to pay acute attention to its young people, listen to their voices, and involve them in the life of the church and community. This book will help congregations understand what is necessary and vitally important in fostering a thriving faith in today's adolescents. As they listened carefully to the voices of the experts, those with lived experiences, the authors took seriously the voices of young adults, not long removed from adolescence, heard what was important for them, and now provide to us, the readers, their insights and their proposal for *"Pressing Forward"* toward a future direction for ministry to and with Black adolescents. If we listen, and if we *Press Forward*, I truly believe the young people entrusted to our care will certainly thrive!

—Rev. Dr. Reggie Blount
Murray H. Leiffer Associate Professor of Formation,
Leadership and Culture Director,
Holy Yearnings, Holy Listening,
Holy Partnerships Young Adult Initiative
Garrett-Evangelical Theological Seminary

NOTES
1. Cornel West, *Race Matters* (Boston: Beacon Press, 1993), 3.
2. Ellis Cose, *The Rage of a Privileged Class: Why are Middle-Class Blacks Angry? Why Should America Care?* (New York: HarperCollins, 1993), 10.

Preface

This book had its genius several years ago as Dr. Denise Janssen and I discussed the dearth of resources that address Black adolescent formation. Each of us, having taught at our respective seminaries for a number of years, were dismayed because we knew the need.

Our conversations led us to decide to do some research together and to see how it might produce a book for use in the classroom for us and the countless others who have yearned for such a resource.

Using the skills we gained from Dr. Margaret Ann Crain during our pursuit of PhD in Christian education and congregational studies at Garrett Evangelical Seminary, Evanston, Illinois, and inspired by the words and encouragement of Dr. Jack Seymour, we embarked on a journey of ethnographic research. Over a period of three to four years we met with groups of Black African American young adults across a wide spectrum of the United States.

As we listened, we heard many similarities in their stories. We decided that the most effective and integral way to tell their stories was to write through my lens, an African American. Why? Dr. Janssen teaches at a predominantly Black seminary, but realizes her perspective is colored by her bias as a person of European descent and all of the privileges that go along with being white in the United States.

On the other hand, as an African American I hear and see with a hermeneutics of suspicion because of my experiences with oppression. Moreover, I have had the privilege for over two decades of being immersed in Christian education, youth ministry, and formation in a predominantly Black denomination. Prior to that I had been a pastor in Black congregations.

Therefore, the voice you hear in this book is mine.

However, Dr. Janssen's contributions to this work are enormous. Not only did she assist in the research, but she served as an editor and a mind of reason throughout the process. Most of all, she was a larger-than-life listening colleague.

As a way of acknowledgment, thanks must be given to all of the Black young adults who we interviewed and all of the Black churches and other Black institutions who allowed us to use their facilities for focus groups and interviews.

Finally, thanks to Freda and Randy, our spouses, who always provide needed encouragement and thoughtful insights.

—Carmichael Crutchfield

Introduction

In a country where Black people have often been rendered invisible, the Black church has made people seen and given men and women a sense of dignity. The Black church has served as the launching pad for civil rights. The Black church has sent thousands of young people to college and provided an avenue for education that otherwise would not have happened. The Black church has given Black people leadership opportunities. The Black church has bestowed community, political power, protection, learning, inspiration, and even recreation to people who were brought to this country to be enslaved.

This book grows out of a deep love for the church, particularly the Black church, and for the amazing, complex, gifted, blessed adolescents who have and are currently growing up in faith in this context. It is the deep desire of both authors to understand the needs and commitments of Black adolescents to develop their relationship with God the Creator. We are both passionate about fostering to flourishing the ways faith is formed in African American adolescents in the Black church.

This work comes from realizing that most Black congregations feel strongly about the faith formation of the youth entrusted to them. It is also true that there are varying levels of understanding when it comes to human development. Congregational values differ in what's most important for people of faith of any age to learn. And not every congregation that claims to love its youth really understands how best to do that. We cannot love what we do not know. And we cannot know someone—even someone we have been familiar with since birth—until we have listened to their hearts and passions and dreams and needs.

Many, if not most, African American churches rely on untrained and underequipped adults to encounter, teach, and form adolescents in the faith. And many African American adolescents have grown into people with a mature faith. To be sure, there is far more than education or training that makes a teacher of youth effective.

However, some African American adolescents struggle to find meaning in church. This may be the result of many factors within the adolescent or the church—something we will explore further in later chapters. This book asks: What are the undergirding factors that foster a flourishing faith in African American adolescents?

Faith formation is a partnership between God's action and human action. God's grace works within persons to deepen their relationship with Jesus Christ through instruction, nurture, and care of the faith community (church) leading them to respond to the enabling work of the Holy Spirit in faithful Christian discipleship. Karen-Marie Yust offers a helpful definition of faith and faithfulness. In doing so, the meaning of discipleship is expanded. Yust says that "faith is a gift from God. It is an act of grace in which God chooses to be in relationship with humanity and it comes to us in and through all our senses. Faithfulness is a human response to God's gift of faith."[1]

Participation in the life of the church forms our lives for Christian discipleship or faithfulness. Our faith is formed through the worshiping, teaching, caring, and serving ministries of the church. We grow in faith by participating in the Christian community. We are developing our Christian identity.

Christian identity means coming to know oneself as a Christian, having assimilated the values, beliefs, and lifestyle of one who professes to be a follower of Jesus Christ. "The purpose of Christian education . . . is to 'build up' or construct communities of faith to praise God and serve neighbors for the sake of the 'emancipatory transformation of the world.'"[2]

At the heart of Christian identity is Christian vocation—love of God and love of neighbor. To be Christian is to commit to a vocation of discipleship, "doing all to the glory of God." The second-century

Church father Irenaeus is credited with saying, "The glory of God is man [or woman] fully alive." How do we really glorify God? When we are alive in God.

Nurturing Christian identity and Christian vocation has been the educational task of the church across the centuries as the church explored ways to pass on the faith to new generations. This has led to a need to give greater emphasis to spiritual formation. Christian faith formation aims to help persons recognize the working of God's grace and their need for repentance. God's work of transformation begins with baptism and initiates the Christian life, while faith formation cultivates human response to God's grace. As one grows in faith, he or she claims what John Westerhoff refers to as "an owned faith as a conversion experience that involves a major change in a person's thinking, feeling, and willing."[3]

Owned faith is lived faith—a witnessing and serving faith. Whether instantaneous or gradual, conversion is a transformative experience through which we come to know God's forgiveness and salvation in Jesus Christ. Christian faith formation intends to share the good news of God's grace in Jesus Christ and help people recognize their need for that grace while learning what it means to be faithful in everyday life. With this book, we hope to offer some insights from our research into the ways churches can foster the kind of owned faith that becomes a lifelong lived faith in the life of the adolescents in their midst.

In a church school class recently one of the members expressed how she has trouble convincing her past-young-adult-age daughter why she should attend church. Her daughter tells her she can "get church on television; therefore, she does not see a reason to attend church." This came as a result of talking about "Jesus being found in our hearts and not constrained to the church." I asked the class, if God is found in our hearts, why do we need to come to church on Sunday? I am of the opinion that many times young people lose interest in "church" because we as adults do a poor job of helping them understand "church." We have failed to help them see the strength that comes from living a life of faithfulness in the presence and with the support of others who are trying to do the same. We have done a poor job of creating an environment where adolescents feel like their presence matters, where they know others in the congregation value them for more than just bragging rights that their church has significant numbers of youth. We have fallen short of creating a worship experience where the encounter with God in worship changes worshipers' hearts and minds—and this has far less to do with drums and light shows than with the authenticity of the experience. In short, we as adults have lost focus or maybe never really understood ourselves.

I have asked adults in seminary classes to give me one compelling reason why someone should come to the church they attend. I have found it difficult to get thoughtful answers from them. I am often left with the impression that some people come to church because it is a socially acceptable thing to do, out of habit, or because of the quality of the "show."

I guess you can say I was raised in the church, but that did not prevent me from not attending church while I was in college. It was the first time I had an option about going to church, and I did not go. In contrast, my son, Chris, who was also raised in the church, went to church every Sunday while in college. I often ask myself what was the difference between the two of us. I have a hunch that the answers to most of my questions lie in the formation of our young people.

In part this is why we wrote a book about the formation of adolescents in the African American church. Helping congregations understand what is important in fostering a vibrant faith in adolescents was a major motivation for this ethnographic study of adolescent faith formation in the Black church. One of the best ways to understand what's important to someone is to ask them, and then listen carefully, so that's what we did. We hope you'll listen in to their responses. Stay tuned!

NOTES

1. Karen-Marie Yust, *Real Kids, Real Faith: Practices for Nurturing Children's Spiritual Lives* (San Francisco: Jossey Bass, 2004), 6.

2. Charles R. Foster, *Educating Congregations: The Future of Christian Education* (Nashville: Abingdon, 1994), 13.

3. John H. Westerhoff III, *Will Our Children Have Faith?* (New York: Seabury, 1976), 89.

Chapter 1

Born Out of Struggle

The Unique Black Church

In some important ways, the existence of the Black church is an act of resistance in and of itself, a miracle of God's grace. The roots of the Black church began to grow during slavery toward the end of the slave trade in the United States, when the religions and cultures of formerly enslaved Africans began to transition and transform. This occurred as the US-born population of enslaved Africans increased, allowing for different African cultures to come together and blend, becoming more distinctly African American.[1] Eventually, while the South was experiencing religious awakenings, many enslaved Africans converted to Christianity, mainly Methodist and Baptist denominations. The message of equality the gospel offered spoke to the issues and passions of enslaved Africans and provided hope for their cause. However, many white slave owners did not take kindly to the idea of enslaved Africans practicing religion on their own, as they feared it would aid in organized attempts at revolt or escape. Thus, many forced their enslaved Africans to attend white-controlled Christian services that preached the importance of obedience to one's masters.

This move on the part of slave owners was an attempt at formation, a very particular kind of formation. In fact, the reality that formation has been used as a tool of oppression serves as a reminder to take care to name the formation being sought. Not all formation is in the best interest of those being formed. Not all formation is liberative, and when formation is not liberative, it does not serve the gospel or the kin-dom. Power and authority figure into seemingly innocuous attempts at formation in faith, and one must always ask about the character of the faith being formed. Navigating issues of formation in the Christian faith required clarity and wisdom on the part of African Americans during this period. The writings of John Jea, an African American preacher in the antebellum South, illustrate the struggle that slaves at the time dealt with in regard to their faith in relation to their daily lives:

> Our labor was extremely hard, being obliged to work in the summer from about two o'clock in the morning, till about ten or eleven o'clock at night, and in the winter from four in the morning, till ten at night. . . . We dared not murmur, for if we did, we were corrected with a weapon an inch-and-a-half thick, and that without mercy, striking us in the most tender parts, and if we complained of this usage, they then took four large poles, placed them in the ground, tied us up to them, and flogged us in a manner too dreadful to behold . . . This was the general treatment which slaves experienced. After our master had been treating us in this cruel manner, we were obliged to thank him for the punishment he had been inflicting on us, quoting that Scripture which saith, "Bless the rod, and him that hat appointed it." But, though he was a professor of religion, he forgot that passage which saith, "God is love, and whoso dwelleth in love dwelleth in God and God in him." And, again, we are commanded to love our enemies; but it appeared evident that his wretched heart was hardened; which led us to look up unto him as our god, for we

did not know him who is able to deliver and save all who call upon him in truth and sincerity. Conscience, that faithful monitor, (which either excuses or accuses) caused us to groan, cry, and sigh, in a manner which cannot be uttered.[2]

In the midst of the drought and devastation of 1865, Black people formed new churches. Before the Civil War, in most parts of the South, enslaved Africans were forbidden to hold services without a white minister present. In the typical plantation church, whites sat in front and enclaved Africans sat or stood in the back. The doctrines preached were infused with the assumption of white supremacy and of servility to this order—more indoctrination than education. It is immediately clear that these efforts were not intended to form Black people in Christian faith, for that would entail modeling a value or characteristic, such as inferiority or superiority, rather than a behavior.

Religious Life of the Enslaved Africans

The religion of those enslaved was both institutional and non-institutional, visible and invisible. There were three ways in which African American worship helped provide the formation of Africans during American slavery: first, in segregated biracial churches where white ministers preached; second, in African American churches such as the African Methodist Episcopal Church founded in 1816; and third, in hidden hush harbors where slaves were free to combine both African and Christian worship practices.[3]

In the hush harbors or brush arbors, enslaved men and women made Christianity truly their own. The religion there was especially sometimes organized and sometimes spontaneous. Formation took place through informal prayer meetings on weeknights. "Preachers licensed by the church and hired by the master were supplemented by slave preachers licensed only by the spirit. Texts from the Bible that most of the enslaved men and women could not read were explicated through the spirituals. Forbidden by the masters to attend church or, in some cases, even to pray risked floggings to attend secret gatherings to worship God."[4]

Newly formed Black churches quickly became the center of the emerging self-led Black communities postwar. Black churches served as community centers and mutual aid societies in addition to their religious role. They fought for the education of Black people and became greenhouses where educational opportunities grew and thrived. To the extent that African American community members held elective office in the first years after the war, their leaders overwhelmingly originated from the churches.

These churches also worked with the Bureau of Refugees, Freedmen, and Abandoned Lands—usually called the Freedmen's Bureau—to create many of the first schools founded to educate African American adults and children after the Civil War. For many in the abolitionist movement, the impulse for education was a natural extension of their agitation for the end of slavery. Most abolitionists engaged in the education of formerly enslaved Africans were young, unmarried, well-educated women from middle-class homes. They carried with them to the South a philosophy of hard-working individualism, mixed with a deeply Christian sense of social responsibility. Southern whites found plenty to complain about in their supposed naïveté and meddlesome ways. A common complaint was that the freed slaves became insolent as the Freedmen's Bureau educated them in the ways of radicalism.

Black churches produced the first generation of political leaders in the Black community, becoming an incubator of courageous and visionary leaders. Hiram Revels is an example of one such leader. Born a free man in North Carolina, he became a preacher and ended up in Natchez, Mississippi, by the late 1860s. According to contemporary accounts, he was impressive enough in intelligence and oratorical ability that the Mississippi State Senate was moved to nominate him for a US Senate seat.[5]

Reading and education were the great desire of the freed slaves, a powerful impulse still present in Black churches. There were old women who wanted to read the Bible before they died. There were mothers who wanted their children to have a better life. All of them studied profusely.

Mentioned earlier, the Freedmen's Bureau was a federal bureau created to assist the freed slaves in their transition to citizenship. Besides providing food rations to prevent starvation, a key focus of the bureau was education. The bureau worked with Black churches to locate suitable teachers, to provide funds for schools, and eventually to create colleges that were heavily focused on the training of future educators and ministers.

After emancipation, Black churches became virtually the only place for African Americans to find refuge. Blacks moved away from the hush harbors to which they had retreated for solace as slaves. Realizing that institutional and implicit racism were insidious even among the best-intentioned abolitionists, it was during this time that a church separation petition was filed by thirty-eight Black members of the predominantly white Fairfield Baptist Church in Northumberland County, Virginia, in 1867. Referring to the new political and social status of African Americans, the petitioners said they wanted to "place ourselves where we could best promote our mutual good" and suggested "a separate church organization as the best possible way." A month later the white members of the church unanimously acceded to the petitioners' request, setting the stage for the creation of the all-Black Shiloh Baptist Church. Led by the Baptists, Black churches spread rapidly throughout the South.[6]

During this period, it was of critical importance to equip Black educators. Accomplishing this in the South of the 1860s was no small feat. In the years after the Civil War, no state in the entire South had a system of universal, state-funded education. With a few exceptions, Southern whites refused to teach African Americans, particularly under the auspices of the despised Freedmen's Bureau. In the immediate aftermath of emancipation, there was a shortage of qualified Black teachers and those willing to teach African American learners. One solution lay in finding educators from the North.

Another solution was the establishment of Black educational institutions. At the end of the Civil War and up through the 1880s, several institutions of higher learning were created. I use the word *created* because in most cases these institutions almost evolved ex nihilo (out of nothing). These institutions came about due to the tenacity of formerly enslaved Africans and their supporters to overcome the tragic evils perpetrated upon Black people during slavery that denied education.[7]

It is well documented that there were certain Black codes that prohibited the slaves from learning to read and write. Black codes were restrictive laws designed to limit the freedom of African Americans and ensure their availability as a cheap labor force after slavery was abolished during the Civil War. Though the Union victory had given some four million slaves their freedom, the question of freed Blacks' status in the postwar South was still very much unresolved. Under Black codes, many states required Blacks to sign yearly labor contracts; if they refused, they risked being arrested, fined, and forced into unpaid labor.[8] These Black codes were the direct cause of irreparable harm inflicted upon Blacks who were denied the right to satisfy the human craving to know and learn.

The strong historical connection between the Black church, education, and adolescents has its genesis in this period in the formation of the Black church. For example, in 1867, two years after the Civil War ended, Augusta Institute was established in the basement of Springfield Baptist Church, the oldest independent African American church in the United States, in Augusta, Georgia. Its purpose was to prepare Black men for the ministry and teaching. Augusta Institute is now known as Morehouse College, a historically Black college in Atlanta, Georgia.[9]

Black churches establishing schools after reconstruction included African Methodist Episcopal, African American Methodist Zion, Baptist, Christian Methodist Episcopal, Presbyterian, and Methodist (even though not entirely Black). During this period, education was highly valued by families for their adolescents, who entered these newly formed colleges and became young adult teachers and preachers at a rapid pace, equipped for both secular and spiritual aspects of the world. Preachers or ministers were often also teachers in elementary and secondary schools. It was typical for students to be taught history, English, and math alongside the Lord's Prayer and the Twenty-third Psalm. It is easy to see how Black students were not so much becoming Christians only on Sundays in the Sunday schools. Rather, every day they were being formed into the likeness of Jesus Christ as Black students were being trained in the essence of what love of neighbor entailed and steeped in moral teaching of right and wrong actions.

Education was much more than satisfying curiosities of the mind. It was the forming of young people—adolescents—into good and productive citizens. Furthermore, it was an opportunity to overcome the social, economic, and personal inequities that Black people had encountered in enslavement.

While a transformation was taking place in the newly integrated public schools, the Black church continued as it had from its inception to promote education—formation of whole people—and saw it as an integral part of its mission. In my denomination, the Christian Methodist Episcopal Church, Bishop Othal Hawthorne Lakey describes it in this way: "Apart from the actual spread of the church itself, education has been the central missional activity of the Christian Methodist Episcopal Church."[10] My home church for years served as a school during the week. Education and religion went hand in hand. Lakey points out that there was no distinction between the secular and the sacred in the historic mission of the church. Education for early CMEs was Christian education in which the basic educational skills were taught but the content was the principles of the Christian religion. "Monday school" was a little different from "Sunday school," as religion was very much a part of the school day. On Sunday, much of the Sunday school time was used in teaching other subjects besides religion, and this was as true for adults as it was for children. Some of the early Sunday school lesson materials of the CME Church had the usual Bible study verses and interpretation, true enough. But they also included the alphabet, spelling, and grammar lessons.[11]

7

Faith Formation in the Black Church, Then and Now

From its inception, the Black church has recognized a singularity to human existence. While respect of elders is a deep value, there is an acknowledged commonality of life experience that runs across generations—a sense of family in the midst of struggle. Making a way for

CARMICHAEL'S STORY: This vein of education continued even under adverse conditions, such as "separate but equal" laws that were designed to keep Black people in an inferior state or condition. In the mid-1960s, when I was in the seventh and eighth grades, I recall being in band at my "Black" school. My fellow band members and I received the discarded band uniforms of the "white" school and then dyed the uniforms to match our school colors. This was necessary because neither our parents nor our school had the resources to purchase uniforms. Most of us were relegated to playing used instruments.

Black children were sent to school by parents who could scarcely afford to make a living for themselves. My father would relate his stories of growing up in the rural South, having been born in 1926. He was forced to end his formal education after he reached the eighth grade. His hands and feet were needed in fields so that his family could survive. I have heard numerous stories that attest to my father's experience.

Education in my upbringing, which was moral from the standpoint that children were taught what was right and wrong, was the business of the church, school, and family. I recall many times seeing how this was acted out. My first-grade teacher's husband, my cousin, was my bus driver, and both were members of my church. The strict rules at home were reinforced from the time I got on the school bus to the time I returned home in the afternoon. For instance, on the bus there was to be no loud talking, hitting, or any sign of disrespect for those in authority (e.g., bus driver the next generation and encouraging its thriving is a foundational principle shared throughout the life cycle. A lifeline runs through the history of the Black church, a sense that it plays a unique role in creating a place and space for cultural values to be transmitted and community to be formed. There is a knowing and a being that are shaped in the doing of the Black church.

and teacher). This education from the first grade until the tenth grade formed the basis for my definition of education: "the preparation to be a good contributing citizen of the society."

You might ask what happened during the remainder of my educational experience, after the tenth grade. Well, beginning in the eleventh grade and forward, my education was not so much about formation as it was about education and indoctrination. When I entered the eleventh grade, suddenly I was surrounded for the first time by people other than Black people as schools began to be desegregated. I contend that alone was good, but along with this new environment came a reduction in rules that had to be followed and the civility they were present to enforce. No longer on the bus was there respect for my cousin, the bus driver. No longer in classrooms did I find consistent expectations of respect for teachers and administrators. I even witnessed my classmates skipping school to go to the lake. I was encouraged to cheat on tests, which was unheard of prior to the eleventh grade. It seemed right and wrong were no longer priorities in the educational process. The bottom line was to make good grades. No longer were the church, school, and family connected. My goal and direction in life were now to be focused on receiving good grades, going to college, and getting a good job. The purpose of school was no longer the formation of young people's lives for the "greater good of society," but for my own individual "greater good." Education had shifted from the community to the individual.

The extended family has been the basis of the Black church from its inception. It is common for the laity of a congregation or even a denomination to address each other as brother or sister. This has been the protocol for pastors in addressing laity. The concept of extended family has played a major role in the faith formation of African American adolescents. This concept has meant that family goes beyond bloodlines and includes all the members of the congregation. Members have taken on the responsibility of literally providing guidance and discipline as needed to children and youth of the congregation. This was more pronounced prior to the integration of schools. I will say more about this in a later chapter.

A STORY FROM CARMICHAEL: As a teenager my older brother and I went out on a Saturday night to a place that we knew was taboo. Unknown to us, one of the adult members of the church was also present, and he questioned our being in such a place. We immediately left the place, thinking we were in the clear. The next day our father inquired about our whereabouts the night before. When we were slow to answer, he told us he knew where we had been. The adult member of our church, our extended family member, had not only challenged us but went on to tell our parents. Interestingly, after schools were integrated in the late 1960s and early 1970s, a new ethos became common. No longer were the discipline and guidance common. African Americans took on more of the attitude of school officials who did not see that all adults had the authority to discipline, challenge, and guide children and youth.

As the broader culture shifts in some important ways, the extended-family role of the Black church becomes more complicated. What was once viewed as an appropriate, gentle touch to refocus a child's attention might now be viewed as an unwelcome touch by a parent who is concerned about others touching her child in any way because of a rightful and growing concern about inappropriate touch. What might once have been understood as a welcome reporting of a child's behavior to a parent might now be received as judgmental criticism and shunned. Recognizing the complications, it still seems clear that this extended family identity of the Black church has played a positive role in the lives of the African American adolescents in this study, as the coming chapters will describe.

Looking Ahead

It is through the lens of a change in the ethos that we listen to the stories of adolescents today who are two to three generations removed from legal segregation but nevertheless often find segregation to be a reality even when it appears not to exist. We further want to listen to these stories to see how African American adolescents' identities are being formed, specifically as they relate to the formation of faith. We listen further to their stories to hear how the relationships of the twenty-first century might be much different from earlier centuries in the Black church. It is our belief that in listening to these stories, we might find a key to understanding faith formation in African American adolescents.

Question: What does history teach us that might help the Black church move forward in the twenty-first century?

NOTES
1. Laurie F. Maffly-Kipp, "An Introduction to the Church in the Southern Black Community," May 2001, Documenting the American South, http://docsouth.unc.edu/church/intro.html.

2. From John Jea, *The Life, History, and Unparalleled Suffering of John Jea, African Preacher* (1811).

3. Albert J. Raboteau, *Slave Religion: The "Invisible Institution" in the Antebellum South* (New York: Oxford University Press, 1978), 212.

4. Ibid.

5. Dan Bryan, "Education and Religion—The Black Community in Reconstruction," February 26, 2012, American History USA, https://www.americanhistoryusa.com/education-religion-Black-community-reconstruction/.

6. The Center for African American Ministries and Black Church Studies (5460 South University Avenue Chicago, IL 60615); Marvin A. McMickle, *An*

Encyclopedia of African American Christian Heritage (Valley Forge, PA: Judson Press, 2002).

7. Shaw and Virginia Union were founded by American Baptist Home Mission Societies and the American Baptist Women's Home Mission Society. Lane College, Miles College, Texas College, and Mississippi Industrial College were founded by the CME Church; Morris Brown College, Allen University, and Paul Quinn College were founded by the AME Church; Livingstone College was founded by the AMEZ Church. These were some of the institutions. Additionally, Paine College was founded by the Methodist Episcopal Church and the CME Church.

8. History.com editors, "Black Codes," June 10, 2010, updated January 21, 2021, History.com, https://www.history.com/topics/Black-history/Black-codes.

9. "Today in Black History: February 18, 1867, the Augusta Theological Institute Was Founded Which Will Later Become Morehouse," February 20, 2020, The Melanin Project, https://www.themelaninproject.org/tmpblog/2020/2/18/today-in-Black-history-february-18-1867-the-augusta-theological-institute-was-founded-which-will-later-become-morehouse.

10. Othal Lakey, *History of the CME Church*, rev. ed. (Memphis: CME Publications, 1996), 438.

11. Ibid., 441.

Chapter 2

Who Am I?

A Complicated Relationship

At the heart of adolescent development is the need for identity formation. This identity development work takes place in some unique ways for adolescents within the context of the African American church. Identify formation is no simple task, but it becomes exponentially more difficult when marginalization plays a significant role. In this chapter, we will explore the particular ways in which African American churches help to form an identity in their adolescent members, with an investigation into identity theory and some views from a postmodern perspective.

At the writing of this chapter, the world is experiencing the COVID-19 pandemic. It is a time of almost overwhelming challenges that require adjustments in every area of life. No one is exempt. The pandemic has taken the world into a maelstrom of adjustments. Almost everyone in school, church, and business has now become partners with Zoom with some level of frustration.

On a Zoom call recently, I heard a colleague lament, "I spent time adjusting the way I was to teach this semester; therefore, I did not have time to do the thing I love to do, i.e., write. I have found it difficult and nearly impossible to work because of all of the changes." On another occasion I heard a colleague say to me in reference to my being a pastor, denominational executive, and a professor at a seminary, "I do not see how you work three jobs and still have time to write." My response was to say, "I don't know either." But deep within my being I believe that it had something to do with the way I was raised and the experiences of making adjustments constantly.

I have often wondered if the DNA of people who are descendants of Africa includes elements of resiliency, perseverance, and the ability to adjust. At the beginning of my junior year in high school, my small all-Black school was forced to merge with six predominantly white schools to become one high school. I went from being in a class of about thirty-five students to about 350 students. I went from ten years of experiencing all-Black faculty, administration, and staff to experiencing minimal Black faculty, administration, and staff. This was an adjustment that I along with thousands of African American adolescents were forced to make during the 1960s and 1970s. I remember a conversation I had in high school with my then best friend, Joseph. We made a pact to take difficult classes and show white people we were able to compete and excel in their dominant environment. We made the adjustment, and both of us succeeded, at least to our satisfaction.

I was the first in my family and, I believe, in my church to go to college. I had no one to coach me or even tell me what college life would be like. My freshman year I was taken in by the freedom college offered, and I thought I was in high school where I could do well without much effort. After receiving the first grade in my life under a B and receiving two D grades, I was awakened and realized freedom came with responsibility and that college required much more effort. I made the necessary adjustments. It seems to me that part of the identity formation of African American youth is the word *adjustment*. It seems it may be due in part to a social culture that has always had to adjust.

One example of the ability of African American youth to adjust to life's challenges is supported by an article by Marjorie Valbrun that states, "HBCUs are getting high student compliance with social distancing and mask wearing and are reporting lower coronavirus infection rates. College leaders partly credit Black college culture—and student awareness of the toll of the pandemic on Black, Latinx and Indigenous communities."[1]

It is my contention that the African American church has had an integral part in forming its adolescents to deal with change and how to make adjustments. Sometimes it is controversial to determine exactly when Africans became Christians, but it is well documented that religion has played a large role in the history of African Americans. Africans who were enslaved hearts, souls, and minds resonated with the biblical message of justice, liberation, and equality. In post-Civil War America, a burgeoning Black church played a key role in strengthening African American communities and in providing key support to the civil rights movement.[2]

For African Americans, the Bible's narrative of the exodus is a cultural touchstone. Since before the Civil War, the story of the Israelites' slavery and deliverance has spurred comparisons with Black people's experiences in the United States. Scripture's importance to the Black population in the US is reflected in Pew Research Center survey data showing that Black people are more likely than most other Americans to read Scripture regularly and to view it as the Word of God. Indeed, more than half of Black people in the US (54 percent)—both Christian and non-Christian—say they read the Bible or other holy Scripture at least once a week outside of religious services, compared with 32 percent of whites and 38 percent of Hispanics, according to data from the 2014 Religious Landscape Study. Indeed, relatively few Black people (24 percent) say they seldom or never read the Bible, compared with 50 percent of whites and 40 percent of Hispanics.[3]

Although the African American church has had and continues to have a great influence on adolescents, identity formation is not limited to the spiritual or religious arena. Emotional development is also taking place in adolescence. This is critical because during this period in a person's life self-concepts are being formed. This is how one believes. At the same time self-esteem is being shaped. This is how people feel about what they believe and especially about themselves.

Like other adolescents, African American youth are developing cognitively. This has been evidenced over the decades when Black youth have been placed side by side with their white counterparts in classrooms. According to the work of Jean Piaget, the cognitive development they are undergoing helps adolescents to think hypothetically about their lives, specifically about the future. They begin to evaluate alternatives, set personal goals, have some introspection, and become capable of making well-considered decisions. Adolescence is a time when young people become more responsible and begin to engage in adult activities such as getting a driver's license, starting to work part-time, and dating more seriously. They are becoming more independent and developing a social conscience. However, some theorists say that the adolescent brain does not process danger well, connecting consequences to actions, so they sometimes can make poor decisions.

"It used to be we as teens would fight it out, but now they shoot at each other." A young adult said these words to me not long ago as we were in dialogue about gun violence. He said, "Man, when I was younger, I did some crazy stuff." He went on to explain that he once climbed through a girl's bedroom window. "I wouldn't dare do something like that now." Teens act on impulse, misread or misinterpret social emotions, get into accidents of all kinds, get involved in fights, or engage in dangerous or risky behavior. Adolescents are less likely to think before they act, think about the consequences of their actions, or change their dangerous or inappropriate behaviors.

Studies show that girls have lower self-esteem often and can really get into making their bodies and faces look a certain way. The culture we live in glamorizes a certain look, and oftentimes adolescent boys and girls become obsessed with "looking good." Studies have shown that boys emotionally may have to learn it is all right to have emotions, but at the same time learn how to manage certain emotions, such as anger. In the program that I started called Enlightened Males, an entire session of the curriculum focuses on dealing with anger. This is necessary because there is a great deal of justified anger.

Cultural aspects of life also play a major part in emotional develop-ment because it becomes a time when ethnicity becomes more impor-tant. This awareness often is more difficult for minorities in society because of negative stereotypes and the lack of positive images in schools and other places they inhabit. I add parenthetically that I have always found it necessary when working with Black youth to ask ques-tions about how they feel about being African American, because of the many negative images sometimes portrayed. More importantly, I have not only asked but also challenged Black boys, especially, to give reasons for feeling positive about being Black in America.

Social development is also an area of development for adolescents. This development comes in the context of family and friends. James Fowler says this is a time when young people are expanding their sphere of influence.[4] Oftentimes in early adolescence, this sphere is ex-panded to the point where family has less influence. As adolescents be-come older, these peers move toward romances. Adolescents engage more and more in activities under the influence of peers. These some-times are good and sometimes can be not so good.

Although the relationships between adolescents and parents lessen, parents still remain important to adolescents. As a matter of fact, stud-ies show that family closeness is a factor in controlling high-risk be-havior from teens, such as smoking, drugs, alcohol, and even sexual activity. My observation over the years in working with Black youth from a variety of venues has been that even youth without strong fam-ily ties can also find extended family in church and community groups that have a tremendous influence on their lives. However, because of increasing independence, there are often conflicts with families and other authority figures. Studies also show that the context of one's community plays a larger role in the social development of adolescents.

Last, there is behavioral development. This is a time of experimen-tation and risk-taking. Erik Erikson emphasized the work of identity formation as central for adolescents, because new decision-making skills and choices are extremely important. It is during behavioral development that young people begin to make real assessments of themselves and seek to gain peer acceptance and respect. This is a fragile time in life. Sexual activity, experimenting with drugs, driving with reckless abandon, and defiance of authority are but a few of the behaviors that can lead to death, but it is difficult to see this as an adolescent who believes he or she is invincible.

Aerika Brittain argues that attaining adaptation, or fit with contextual demands, may be particularly challenging for African American youth because issues of race may complicate the search for an adaptive identity. For African Americans, adolescence is also a time when they begin to consider themselves in regard to race and ethnicity.[5] Beverly Christine Daniel Tatum, a psychologist and educator who focuses on racial identity development in teenagers, suggests that in early adolescence individuals first begin to differentiate friendships by ethnic group and to show increased group-esteem and ethnic exploration.[6] Therefore, African American youth must define themselves in relation to the social status and meaning of their racial and ethnic group.[7]

Adolescence is in many ways a fragile time in all areas of development. Young people need guidance and communal support. It is also a crucial time for leadership formation in adolescents. Although I am aware this is not exclusively critical for African American adolescent males, I have made it my primary interest for reasons outlined in Chapter 1. Furthermore, the need is highlighted by our former President of the United States Barack Obama, when he wrote as a US Senator the foreword of *The State of Black America* in 2007. In that publication he said, "In some cities, more than half of all Black boys do not finish high school, and, by the time they are in their thirties, almost six in ten Black high school dropouts will have spent time in prison."[8]

Adolescents generally, and adolescent males specifically, have a myriad of choices. It is time for them developmentally to be independent, given a great deal of freedom and responsibility, and they have a tremendous need for communal support. Many of them are missing parents, either physically, mentally, socially, emotionally, and behaviorally, in their lives. Studies show that adolescents who have the closeness of adults in their lives develop with less risk-taking and unhealthily decisions, such as drugs, alcohol, and dangerous sexual activity.

Question: How do you explain the impact of anger concerning Black adolescents?

NOTES

1. Marjorie Valbrun, "Hitting Close to Home," September 24, 2020, Inside Higher Ed, https://www.insidehighered.com/news/2020/09/24/hbcus-experiencing-better-student-compliance-pandemic-restrictions-other.

2. David Masci, "Five Facts about the Religious Lives of African Americans," February 7, 2018, Pew Research Center, https://www.pewresearch.org/fact-tank/2018/02/07/5-facts-about-the-religious-lives-of-african-americans/.

3. Jeff Diamant, "Blacks More Likely Than Others in U.S. to Read the Bible Regularly, See It as God's Word," May 7, 2018, Pew Research Center, https://www.pewresearch.org/fact-tank/2018/05/07/Blacks-more-likely-than-others-in-u-s-to-read-the-bibleregularly-see-it-as-gods-word/.

4. Thomas Armstrong, "The Stages of Faith According to James W. Fowler," June 12, 2020, American Institute for Learning and Human Development, https://www.institute4learning.com/2020/06/12/the-stages-of-faith-according-to-james-w-fowler/.

5. Aerika S. Brittain, "Understanding African American Adolescents' Identity Development: A Relational Developmental Systems Perspective," *Journal of Black Psychology* 38, no. 2 (May 2012): 172–200, https://www.researchgate.net/publication/233931724_Understanding_African_American_Adolescents%27_Identity_Development_A_Relational_Developmental_Systems_Perspective.

6. B. D. Tatum, *Why Are All the Black Kids Sitting Together in the Cafeteria?: And Other Conversations about Race* (New York: Basic Books, 1997).

7. Brittain.

8. National Urban League, *The State of Black America: Portrait of the Black Male* (Silver Spring, MD: Beckham's Group, 2007).

Chapter 3

Adolescence 101

As I sit in my seminary office contemplating how to prepare the next video for an asynchronous class during the global pandemic on the theme of this week's session, "Stages of Development in Adolescents," my mind runs backward and forward. As I reflect upon my own adolescence along with the adolescent adventures of my two now-adult children, I wonder, with the dawning of my grandchildren's teen years, what adventures might they have. My mind rolls back to dialogue with youth in the church and various communities over the last thirty years. I flash forward to conversations I am about to have with two teens who have just begun to accept their calling from God.

As a pastor and a community activist I have seen adolescents face challenges in various ways. I recall working with youth when I had no experience prior to my children becoming teenagers. More often than not, this is the case among those who work with adolescents, particularly in small membership congregations. In this chapter I will explore and define adolescence, as well as address identity and faith development. I will specifically give attention to what it means to be a Black teenager in America.

Generally, it is understood that adolescence is the time between puberty and when the legal adult status is attained. Adolescence can be a time of both confusion and encounter with seemingly unlimited options. Markers of this stage of transition include desire and work to establish independence and identity. This desire and work to establish identity can cause a relatively egocentric perspective on life, something that usually abates with age. Adolescents tend to focus on themselves and believe that everyone else—from a best friend to a distant crush—is focused on them, too. They may grapple with insecurities and feelings of being judged. Relationships with family members often take a back seat to peer groups, romantic interests, and appearance, which teens tend to perceive as increasingly important during this time. The transition to adolescence can naturally lead to anxiety about physical development, evolving relationships with others, and one's place in the larger world. Mild anxiety and other challenges are typical, but serious mental health conditions may also emerge during adolescence, which are sometimes related to hormone levels.

In addition, Black adolescents' development is affected by racism that is a "system of structuring opportunity and assigning value based on the social interpretation of how one looks (which is what we call 'race') that unfairly disadvantages some individuals and communities, unfairly advantages other individuals and communities, and saps the strength of the whole society through the waste of human resources."[1] Black teens might experience different types of racism. Sometimes they will experience individual racism. Perhaps white people stared at them with hostility, as though they did not belong. Maybe someone called them a racial slur. Others experience racism through institutions or policies. For example, they might be walking through an area where mostly white people live and get questioned by white people about why they are there. This might happen even when the Black teen lives in that neighborhood. Still others experience cultural racism. This may show up in media reports. For instance, when the news reports a crime, there's often "a focus on negative attributes if it's a Black person." Perhaps the Black teen will be described as having a "dark past." In contrast, a white teen who commits a crime might be described as "quiet" or "athletic."

The social environment in which youth are raised shapes adolescent development. As a result of the pervasive racism and near-constant micro-aggressions, Black youth specifically are traumatized in ways they consciously do not know. Traumatized youth are especially impacted by homelessness; school failure; addiction; apathy; gang involvement; police brutality and racial profiling; child-care crises; unemployment; violence in schools, neighborhoods, and families; parental neglect; excessive consumption; hyper-sexuality and unplanned pregnancy; the militarization of public space; the proliferation of weapons; and general alienation.

In the midst of all of the aforementioned social crises faced by adolescents, they face an "identity crisis," a term coined by Erik Erikson in 1963. He describes his theory in his work on the *Stage of Adolescence, Identity, Identity Crisis* that is part of his psychosocial theory of development.

In the fifth stage of Erikson's theory, identity versus role confusion, he addresses the development of adolescents. He writes that new opportunities, experiences, and changes to the body-mind in stage five are crucial to adolescents' sense of who they are and have a considerable bearing on their adult years.[2] Psychologists have long argued that there is body-mind integration. Psychologist Joaquin Selva explains it this way:

> The reasoning for this stems from the idea that physical conditions affect mental health, and mental conditions affect physical health. Unlike desires or dreams, our thoughts and emotions don't only exist in the mind. Feelings are, well, actual and physical feelings. For examples, people get "butterflies in the stomach" onstage or on a first date, while others who anger easily are described as "hot-headed." And depression actually acts like physical pain or neurochemical level. The body holds your physical health and your ability to function. For example, even the little actions like walking and the fine movements of your fingers depend on a healthy body. But the mind

houses your spirit and your motivation to function. These days, we have evidence that mental and physical health are so related to each other.[3]

On the developmental path from childhood stages to adulthood, the adolescent period provides space for a valuable and in-depth exploration of beliefs, goals, and values while searching for personal identity and a sense of self. This transition is crucial to the individual's growth "between the morality learned by the child, and the ethics to be developed by the adult."[4] Adolescents begin moving toward adulthood, becoming increasingly independent in their decision-making and beginning to try on emerging identities as they consider careers, family, friends, and their place in society.

Ethics versus Morality and Racial Discrimination

In Erikson's statement about the transition from childhood morality to adult ethics described earlier, we are prompted to ask, "What do we mean by morality and ethics? What are some particular factors for Black teens?" People often use the two words interchangeably. They are not synonyms, but historically they have often been used in that manner.

Defining the distinction between morality and ethics is a lifelong process. Some define morality as a sense of right or wrong on the personal level, while ethics are right and wrong at the societal level. Others believe that, while moral values are our sense of wrong, ethics are our morals in action; in other words, ethics are the actions we take and systems we make to take action according to our morals. What is clear is that moral values are deeply held personal beliefs, and they help us know how to act with other people in the world.[5]

Ethics is normative and imperative—it deals with what someone ought to do. Morality describes what someone is actually doing. This is a significant distinction to make, particularly in the context of the Black church and Christianity because the two concepts are so often confused, merged, and blended.

An example of how this affects Black teens developmentally can be found in the context of racial discrimination. As adolescents are in the midst of identity crisis and developing a sense of self, Black teens are denied access to those things needed for development based on the moral values or deeply held personal beliefs that inform how those in power use their power to discriminate against other people, that is, Black and brown people. An example of this is when it would be important for African American adolescents to begin to claim their own sense of agency and challenge unjust and unlawful treatment by police officers but face too great a threat to their lives and well-being, thus arresting development of agency. This is an example of institutional racism. Defined initially by political activists Stokely Carmichael and Charles Vernon Hamilton in 1967, the concept of institutional racism came into the public sphere in 1999 through the Macpherson Inquiry into the racist murder of Black teenager Stephen Lawrence. Institutional racism is defined as "processes, attitudes and behaviour(s) which amount to discrimination through unwitting prejudice, ignorance, thoughtlessness and racist stereotyping which disadvantage minority ethnic people."[6]

At a time in their lives when Black adolescents need to focus on exploration of identity, those Black adolescents are often tangled in the various expressions of racism so deeply embedded in the larger culture. Confusing what should be understood to be issues of morality (personal beliefs) with issues of ethics (the actions we take and the systems we make on a societal level) is central to this problem. Confusing them allows for justification of the kind of marginalization and discrimination against people of color that becomes so developmentally disruptive for Black teens.

Black teenagers experience daily racial discrimination, including harassment online, which can lead to negative mental health effects, according to a Rutgers researcher. A study published in *the Journal of Applied Developmental Psychology* examined how often Black teens experience racial discrimination each day—either personally or vicariously and online or offline.[7] The researchers surveyed 101 Black youth between ages thirteen and seventeen from predominantly Black neighborhoods in Washington, DC, each day for two weeks about their experiences with racial discrimination and measured changes in their depressive symptoms across that period. Those 101 Black teens reported more than 5,600 experiences of racial discrimination in total during those two weeks—an average of more than five experiences per day. And this is just what they remembered and reported.

> This research reflects what researchers and activists have asserted for years: Black adolescents are forced to face antiBlack microaggressions on a daily basis. Importantly, this study expands the research on the many ways that discrimination happens, whether it is being teased by peers, asked to speak for their racial group in class or seeing a racist post on social media, said lead author Devin English, an assistant professor at Rutgers School of Public Health.[8]

The experiences reported in the study, which ranged from teasing about physical appearances, such as the wearing of hair naturally, to more explicit forms of discrimination like seeing jokes about their race online and witnessing a family member or friend being treated poorly due to their race or ethnicity.

"Racial teasing is important because it is one of the most common ways adolescents communicate about race," English noted. "Critically, young people and adults, such as teachers, often see this teasing as harmless and choose not to address it. Our results, however, show several types of racial teasing are harmful for Black adolescents."[9] For example, a Black adolescent might be asked by a white adolescent, "Why do you not like chocolate? Is it because it looks like you?" Another example is the use of symbols, voice, video, images, or text and graphic representations that denigrate Black people.

Black adolescents' experience of racism comes in less evident, harder to pinpoint ways, too. Black teens give witness to the experience of having their work valued less or having their academic ability or intelligence questioned more. They report having less access to advanced placement high-school courses that might help them succeed in college—even being steered away from more challenging or college preparatory classes by teachers and counselors. Some describe bias in career counseling. Each of these incidents wears on the psyche and self-worth of African American adolescents. "Years of scientific study have shown us that, when children's stress response systems remain activated at high levels for long periods, it can have a significant wear-and-tear effect on their developing brains and other biological systems. This can have lifelong effects on learning, behavior, and both physical and mental health."[10]

African American adolescents who experience continual micro-aggressions and incidents of race-based discrimination are among those most at risk of these very real effects on their physical and mental health. The study goes on to observe: "A growing body of evidence from both the biological and social sciences connect this concept of chronic wear and tear to racism. This research suggests that constant coping with systemic racism and everyday discrimination is a potent activator of the stress response. This may help us understand the early origins of racial disparities in chronic illness across the lifespan."[11]

The impacts of racism don't stop with physical and mental health but expand to include the basic processes of human development in ways that are often invisible to people who are not Black or people of color. In the adolescent stage of Erikson's developmental (psychosocial) theory, adolescents either find the support they need to succeed in understanding their identity and develop a coherent self or become mired in indecision, unable to form a personal sense of identity. Unhelpful pressure from culture, peers, and family can leave adolescents struggling with a weaker sense of self and identity—sometimes this impacts their lives for many years. If continual experiences with racism can impact Black adolescents this deeply, it is clear that racism needs to be addressed as the public health issue it is. Churches, schools, families, and our larger culture need to seek ways to ensure that adolescents find appropriate support and encouragement as they develop in order to counteract racism's toxic effects.

Sharing in the Historic Struggle

One way Black adolescents have made meaning of the seemingly senseless impacts of racism has been through active resistance—protest, social activism, working to eliminate unjust laws and enact more just ones. In this way, generations are connected in the Black church in the historic struggle for justice. Black teens can and should help shape the future of justice-seeking, and we as adults need to listen to them. It doesn't have to be the same action that was taken in the past. We all need to find new ways of taking action, as evidenced by the impact of COVID-19 on protests during the pandemic. Today, teens use hashtags, apps, and other methods to pursue racial justice. Even though there are new methods of protest, we must not lose sight of the fact that historically, Black teens have been involved in social justice.

Those who reflect on the civil rights movement of the 1960s recognize that marches and meetings were attended by teens, young adults, and even children. In some cases, they faced violence and imprisonment as a result of their passionate engagement of powers intent on maintaining an unjust status quo. Activist Joyce Ladner points to the strong support of her elders in shaping her future path: "The Movement was the most exciting thing that one could engage in. I often say that, in fact, I coined the term, the 'Emmett Till generation.' I said that there was no more exciting time to have been born at the time and the place and to the parents that movement, young movement, people were born to . . . I remember so clearly Uncle Archie who was in World War I, went to France, and he always told us, 'Your generation is going to change things.'"[12]

In the wake of George Floyd's brutal murder at the hands of Minneapolis police in 2020, protesters took to the streets across the world. Young protesters described the obstacles they faced in having their voices heard, "from distrust and dismissal from adults; to co-optation;

to attrition by graduation, infighting, or simply other obligations as students." Zachary Jason writes in Harvard's *Ed.* magazine that those protesters continued to lead as social activists fighting for equality and justice. Today, many are at the forefront of the Black Lives Matter movement.[13] Young Black protesters do not always feel that they are part of the historic struggle for justice that has marked the Black church throughout its history. It is not that protest is not about justice, but that it is not as attached to the back church as it has been historically. For example, the protests in Minneapolis and around the United States were about justice but were initiated and empowered outside the church. In our research, we heard from youth who felt unsupported and dismissed by their elders, those same elders whose ways of striving for justice are not so different from the methods employed today. How much more important could it be for Black youth, in this moment, to feel supported by their churches, by their elders? Understanding themselves as part of the historic struggle often led by the Black church could empower them to do and be all God is calling them to be.

Faith Development

Meanwhile, still in my office, I move to the computer and begin to write notes to myself as I think about grandchildren. I move to my bookshelf and pick up the book that has been on my mind. It is John Westerhoff's classic, *Will Our Children Have Faith?* I turn to the section referencing stages of faith. I turn my focus to the stage he labels Searching Faith.

> Faith development reaches a crucial junction when one becomes aware that personal beliefs or experience may no longer be exactly the same as those of the group, or when a person begins to question some of the commonly held beliefs or practices. This occurs as one naturally recognizes that his or her faith is formed more by others (parents, peers, congregation, etc.) than by personal conviction. The decision must

be faced whether or not to develop, express, and accept responsibility for a personal interpretation of one's religion as over against accepting that which may be viewed as a group's interpretation. Often there is experimentation in which persons try out alternatives or commit themselves to persons or causes which promise help in establishing personal conviction and active practice of one's faith.[14]

This leads me to explore the meaning of faith. Faith is described as a belief in something beyond one's self. Religion, or being a part of a faith community, can offer support among people with similar faith experiences. Attending church and relying on faith have long been mainstays in the African American community.[15] Both faith and the church have been traditional forms of social and familial involvement for African Americans.[16]

Two teenage members in a church I once served as pastor responded to the invitation to Christian discipleship by coming to the front of the congregation. In my tradition this was a strong expression of faith, especially since the teenagers also desired to be baptized. They both said they now had faith in Jesus Christ. The two young females had been attending church on a regular basis for more than three years. They came to church school and sang in the choir. I explained to them I attended church many years because I came to believe in Jesus. Some have said that faith is caught as much as it is taught as they think about the importance of putting ourselves in the place where we might be influenced to believe.

My work with Black teens informs my understanding of the importance of integration of religion and spirituality in every aspect of adolescents' lives as critical for the development of a healthy identity and a healthy faith. In fact, a common ritual in many ethnic churches is a rite of passage custom that ensures an indoctrination of cultural, spiritual, and humanity expectations. The Enlightened Males program that I mention in Chapter 7 is an example.

The Role of the Church in Faith Development

The role that the Black church plays in faith development is multi-faceted. It serves as a safe haven that temporarily protects African Americans from the cruel realities of a nation filled with discrimination, racism, and mistreatment. My parents were deliberate in providing such a safe harbor for their children. The Black church provides a place where people who are otherwise oppressed can find a voice and dignity among their own. The Black church is a shelter that gives a sense of belonging, security, and power to its members. Historically, this has been true for Black men. Subjected to derogatory name-calling all week long, on Sunday Black men could be addressed as Mr. or Bro. or Deacon. Today, the Black church has taken on additional outreach responsibilities, especially for its youth. Tutoring, conferences, rites of passage, essay and rhetorical contests, concerts, Black college tours, childcare, health education, and employment preparation are just a few of the Black churches' outreach programs.

The church, community, and family work in harmony to provide a solid moral foundation for African American teens. Lawrence Kohlberg, in describing his theory of moral development, stated, "Adolescents need to have specific intellectual and social experiences in order to advance to succeeding levels and stages of moral reasoning." He pointed out varying degrees and levels of principled thinking within each of the stages that inspired youth toward moral behavior. Further, he claimed that "the social experiences of adolescents can serve as an enhancement toward a higher level of moral behavior."[17]

The church can act as a stage on which to practice moral behavior. Historically, Black churches have provided various experiences that support families economically, spiritually, socially, and culturally through customs unmatched by other social institutions. Other experiences, such as leadership roles, ushering, reciting, singing in the choir, reading announcements, and learning church protocol may also serve as conduits of moral thinking for youth.

The church has a "village opportunity" to provide positive experiences for youths. Traditionally, churches in the African American community have served as places of worship and education, worship, civic development, political participation, and worship and community mobilization.

Question: How does racism affect the faith development of Black adolescents?

NOTES

1. Maria Trent, Danielle C. Dooley, and Jacqueline Dougé, "The Impact of Racism on Child and Adolescent Health," *Pediatrics* 148, no. 2 (August 2019), https://pediatrics.aappublications.org/content/144/2/e20191765.

2. Jeremy Sutton, "Erik Erikson's Stages of Psychosocial Development Explained," July 5, 2021, Positive Psychology, https://positivepsychology.com/erikson-stages/.

3. Joaquin Selva, "Mind-Body Integration: Training Attention for Physical and Mental Health," June 25, 2021, Positive Psychology, https://positivepsychology.com/body-mind-integration-attention-training/.

4. Sutton.

5. "What Are Some Examples of Moral Values?", May 27, 2020, Reference, https://www.reference.com/world-view/examples-moral-values-1ba762d2bd5c25b3?ad_dirN&qo_serpIndex&o=740005.

6. "Structural Racism and How It Works," June 30, 2021, The Conversation, https://theconversation.com/structural-racism-what-it-is-and-how-it-works-158822.

7. Devin English, Sharon F. Lambert, Brendisha M. Tynes, Lisa Bowleg, Maria Cecelia Zea, and Lionel C. Howard, "Daily Multidimensional Racial Discrimination among Black U.S. American Adolescents," *Journal of Applied Developmental Psychology* 66 (January–February 2020), https://doi.org/10.1016/j.appdev.2019.101068.

8. Patti Verbanas, "Black Teens Face Racial Discrimination Multiple Times Daily, Suffer Depressive Symptoms as a Result," December 16, 2019, Medical Express, https://medicalxpress.com/news/2019-12-Black-teens-racial-discrimination-multiple.html/.

9. Ibid.

10. A. T. Forde, D. M. Crookes, S. F. Suglia, and R. T. Demmer, "The Weathering Hypothesis as an Explanation for Racial Disparities in Health: A Systematic Review," *Annals of Epidemiology* 33 (2019): 1–18.e3.

11. A. T. Geronimus, M. Hicken, D. Keene, and J. Bound, "'Weathering' and Age Patterns of Allostatic Load Scores among Blacks and Whites in the United States," *American Journal of Public Health* 96, no. 5 (2016): 826–33; B. S. McEwen, "Protective and Damaging Effects of Stress Mediators," *New England Journal of Medicine* 338, no.3 (1998): 171–79.

12. "Youth in the Civil Rights Movement," Civil Rights History Project, Library of Congress, https://www.loc.gov/collections/civil-rights-history-project/articles-and-essays/youth-in-the-civil-rights-movement/.

13. Christopher Rim, "How Student Activism Shaped the Black Lives Matter Movement," June 4, 2020, *Forbes*, https://www.forbes.com/sites/christopher-rim/2020/06/04/how-student-activism-shaped-the-black-lives-matter-movement/?sh=d1d87bb4414a.

14. John H. Westerhoff III, *Will Our Children Have Faith?* (New York: Seabury Press, 1976), 96.

15. J. S. Mattis, "African American Women's Definitions of Spirituality and Religiosity," *Journal of Black Psychology* 26, no. 1 (2000): 101–22.

16. S. F. Hamilton, "An Ecological Approach to Adolescent Development and School," *Human Ecology Forum* 12 (1982): 2–6; C. Eric Lincoln and Lawrence H. Mamiya, *The Black Church in the African American Experience* (Durham, NC: Duke University Press, 1990).

17. Lawrence Kohlberg, "Moral Development and the Education of Adolescents," in *Adolescents and the American High School*, ed. R. F. Purnell (New York: Holt, Rinehart, and Winston, 1970).

Chapter 4

The Core of the Black Church

Praise and Prayer and Proclamation

When we asked groups of young adult African American women and men about their experience growing up in or with ties to the Black church, we heard about many cultural and family ties. Stories emerged about choir as a Black church distinctive in that there was something special about being treated like an adult alongside other adults in the church. We heard that singing in the choir was special in other ways, too—for instance, many times, choir rehearsal becomes a testimonial or worship moment as people feel the Spirit. We heard about the arts—things like mime and praise dance—that made the experience unique. For many in our focus groups, their earliest memories were of singing in a children's choir or using flowing pieces of cloth or ribbons in praise dances that were really just movements to music. We heard about white greasepaint and gloves to mime the gospel stories. We heard about the importance in the community of dressing up in one's best—for some, this still just feels right while others have come to view this practice through a more critical lens. We heard about tables filled with food at church dinners and funeral repasts. We watched faces fill with recognition when one person began a story about the usher board or a church mother or Sunday school, and others picked up a similar story from their own experience. It was almost as if the members of our focus groups had lived the same childhoods.[1]

Pervasive was a sense that these growing-up years were filled with family—biological, but for sure church family. And the family was used in the most richly textured way to describe an experience mixed in its blessing at times. Church family that was messy, just like biological families sometimes are. Church officers who said harsh words to others and sometimes intimidated other people. People they knew who had experienced abuse at the hands of pastors or church leaders. Being celebrated for making the honor roll, given awards for sports and other accomplishments, and "benched" until they were old enough to offer gifts deemed meant for "grown folks."

What we heard in the focus groups develops into definitions of worship based on the experiences and needs of those who were teens not many years removed. This is how we heard the definitions coming forth:

> Worship is freedom where we surrender to be healed; singing; a lifestyle. It is an expression of your relationship with God that causes one to reflect and to be touched. Worship is a relationship with God in the everyday thing. Worship is not putting a handle on the Holy Spirit and becoming too structural. Worship is passionate and appealing to everyone. It is expressive and at the same time knowing God's full presence. It is a feeling that makes you run down the aisle and shout. Worship is not the standard method and is not short. It is getting off a program.

> Worship is being blessed by the preacher with a strong word from God. It is a time of prayer for all where it means leading others in prayer and being in prayer for oneself. It is a praise service where shouting and dancing occur. Worship is totally letting go

and letting God. Worship is what you do to release the stress and to be free. It is being connected to God and one another.

Worship is music and good singing. Worship is community and family where each part is important, therefore, worship must be prepared or planned. Worship is participation and unity among those who worship.

In one focus group, a young adult we will call Angela (all names are pseudonyms) told about how she's overwhelmed with thankfulness during praise and worship sometimes, thinking, "Yes, God has been so good." Tony agreed that music is powerful for him in worship, particularly when it feels like a certain song touches something he's experiencing. When applying for job after job, he felt affirmed that God had chosen him despite the rejections he was receiving. Gina offered that sometimes the words of a song will speak to something she hasn't even spoken aloud or admitted to herself, which feels like a Spirit connection.

We also heard about Christian practices—worship, prayer, music, preaching, testimony—and the central place of worship in the life of the Black church and its members. Faithful grandmothers and big mamas who prayed fervently, even in the face of impossible odds and every indication that what they prayed for would not come to be. Music—hymns, spirituals, and contemporary songs—offered a lingering soundtrack of encouragement as worshipers went out from the church and into their weeks. Songs like "Waymaker" and "I Need You to Survive" that bring a tangible feeling of God's presence were noted along with the emotion they evoke. There were stories about testimonies—not the predictable kind that do little more than brag, but genuine, heartfelt stories of God's activity—and a story that came at just the right time for a young man who was ready to give up on life.

Another young adult, Pandora, confessed that she didn't really understand all of what was going on during the worship service as an adolescent. She remembers clearly passing notes during the worship service on the back row, in fact. But she also gives witness to the time when she claimed a connection to "her church"—and identifying that something must have soaked in all those times she wasn't paying attention.

Manda remembers hearing church mothers pray, particularly at prayer meetings early in the morning. Hearing their prayers and the depth of their faith, then hearing testimonies the next week about experiences that grew out of those prayers is what captured her. She describes faith in her life as more caught than taught, and the prayers of the church mothers were where she identified catching faith. Even as a seminary graduate, she identifies this experience as pivotal for her.

Others pointed to the preacher with whom they had a flesh-and-blood relationship as someone who became a spiritual guide and parent figure or called out something in them or challenged them to be more than they imagined for themselves.

TERRELL TOLD US: What could I say? She lived in another state, I couldn't be there for her physically, and no number of warm words was going to do the trick. She needed comfort, she needed direction, she needed restoration, but most of all, she needed healing in her heart. I had recently been through my own season of darkness, but God had begun to heal my heart in a huge way. Through my own journey of restoration, I was learning that deep heart healing in the midst of inner turmoil can come to us in one of the most surprising, unexpected ways—through worshiping God.

These are the words of a young adult male speaking about his sister's need for healing.

One young adult from one focus group, Melvin, told me about the importance of worship as a time to heal. He talked about how he had been through a lot in his short life. He talked about the death of his younger brother and how much pain that still causes him. He said worship heals, but it takes time. "When I am praising the Lord, I some-times lose track of time and even awareness of my location," he ex-plained. Listening to other young adults speaking about growing up as Black adolescents in the church was good when given freedom.

I have had several opportunities to observe Black youth in worship, for I have been the director of four Connectional Youth and Young Adult Conferences for the Christian Methodist Episcopal Church. What I have learned is that when twenty-five hundred youth are given the freedom to worship, they are very expressive and animated. Time does not seem to be an issue. I have experienced shouting, dancing, and singing during worship. What may be surprising are the responses I have seen the proclamation of the gospel from preachers. It is out of this freedom that youth often respond to an invitation to Christian dis-cipleship after the sermon. Many come seeking prayer; some come for healing; others come to accept Jesus Christ as their Savior. And even others come to accept the call to preach.

I have also experienced the worship of smaller numbers of youth in the same manner. In the mid-1990s, when the use of projectors and screens was not a usual way of worship, we transported about sev-enty-five youth from different parts of Tennessee to our church, where we had two projectors and two screens set up. We created a worship time and space for these Black youth that none of them had experi-enced. It took about fifteen minutes for the participants to feel free. Conversations among them later made us aware they were not accus-tomed to having freedom in worship. We gave the youth permission to express themselves as they were moved. We led them in shouting, singing, and dancing. I preached a sermon from the back of the church, and we gave all of them an opportunity to come forward to express their thoughts about God. My colleague and I learned the following things from that experience.

1. Youth who are accustomed to attending church like to worship God. Young people want to have opportunities with expressions like praise dances and mime.

2. Youth want authentic expressions of worship. Freedom in worship is the ability to worship with all that youth feel God has given them and can be different from what adults receive.

3. Youth will express themselves, if given permission. During mime youth might find themselves giving expressions that are hard for adults to relate.

4. Youth love God just as adults do. Youth are looking for mentors who will accept their love of God.

5. Youth are willing to try new things. Youth want to act out Scriptures, dance, mime, and go beyond the normal worship expressions.

We also learned some things about adults. One, sometimes the view of youth ministry is limited to entertainment. Two, worship is narrowly conceived and planned. Three, adult leaders do not invest enough effort, money, and time into youth ministry.

What we heard throughout our focus groups is that worship brings life to the core of our being.

> When there seems to be no hope and all has been taken away, worship. It really helps. Listen to worship songs, or sing with some worship music you like, or go to a church with a good worship leader, or worship in prayer. I don't really know why it helps so much, just do it, it works. Just fall face down and worship. It's crazy, it's absurd, it does not make logical sense, but God honors it and it's been deeply healing to me. Somehow makes things right. Our hearts need it. God's heart loves it.

Teens, Worship, and Faith Formation

Sharon Vellema says that worship plays a formative role in the faith development of young people.[2] In *Shaped by God*, Robbie Castleman writes, "Life is liturgy. Life has patterns that shape us more and for a lot longer than we ever realize. It is no wonder that liturgy—the pattern of corporate worship—shapes our faith formation more than we ever realize."[3] Nowhere is this more evident than in the life of a teen. Yet many church leaders, youth group leaders, and Christian school chapel coordinators struggle to find effective ways to involve young people in worship.

There is a need for Black churches to ask some important questions about themselves. These questions should be designed to discover the impact worship has on the life of youth and the role of corporate worship in the life of a young person. The Black church is challenged to see how to involve youth in planning and leading worship and to know the time commitment needed to do these things. Ultimately, church leaders have to determine if it is worth the time and effort.

Allowing and encouraging teens to participate in leadership roles during worship services engages young people in a way that can be transformative. In "Youth, Worship, and Faith Formation: Findings from a National Study," the following is stated:

> The most consistent predictor of youth's religiosity was their experience leading worship by doing any of the following: singing or playing an instrument; participating in drama or pageants; leading the congregation in prayer or reading; serving as an acolyte or altar boy/girl; teaching a lesson or meditation or sermon; giving testimony; and serving as usher or greeter or collecting offerings. Youth who reported having done several of these activities also reported higher rates of church attendance, personal prayer, Scripture reading, and volunteer work. In addition, they reported a greater influence of religious teachings on their "big decisions," a stronger commitment to their faith tradition, a stronger commitment to marry within their tradition, and a greater desire for others to know about their faith commitment.[4]

It is important that Black churches consider how to most effectively include youth in the planning and execution of worship. It must be noted that not all youth sing and play musical instruments. Even those who are engaged musically may find themselves excluded from all aspects of worship. This exclusion includes the decision-making of the church. This is a result of possibly the old adage that "children are to be seen and not heard." Also, it may be the result that many older adults have trouble acknowledging the growth of children to adolescents.

When choosing meaningful roles for youth, the entire corporate worship experience in a church must be considered. When God's people gather together in worship, they hear a call to worship; they sing songs of praise and adoration; they engage in a time of confession and listen to God's assurance of forgiveness. The worshipers listen to the word of the Lord spoken and respond to that word. Finally, congregants receive God's blessing at the conclusion of worship. Teens can be involved in many if not all of these aspects of worship. Involving teens in every area of worship, whether in corporate worship with the entire church or in a youth group setting, promotes faith formation in young people. Inviting teens to take on leadership responsibilities prepares them to be active and healthy members of churches in their adult years.

It is my contention that the involvement of youth in worship is faith formation and as a result these youth will remain active in the church in their adult years. "There is no more important community gathering than the Sunday liturgy which telescopes the understandings of life and the preferred ways of life of those who celebrate together. To cease worshiping is to lose faith. To transmit faith to the next generation is to include them as participants in all the community's rituals."[5]

I argue that so many active youth in the church become inactive later because they lack formation. I define formation as the nurturing that takes place in the lives of people that assists persons to practice wholeheartedly the love of God and neighbor. Worship is one of the places formation can happen. It then is important that adolescents learn about worship. Teens need to learn about worship: why we worship, how we worship, and the purpose of worship. Meeting with young people to study and plan worship is an important mentoring opportunity for adults and youth alike.

In the broadest possible sense, they need to learn "articulacy." In *Soul Searching*, the authors state:

> It seems to us that religious educators need to work much harder on articulation. It was also astonishing how many Christian teens, for example, were comfortable talking generally about God but not specifically about Jesus. Philosophers like Charles Taylor argue that inarticulacy undermines the possibilities of reality. So for instance, religious faith, practice, and commitment can be no more than vaguely real when people cannot talk much about them. Articulacy fosters reality. A major challenge for religious educators of youth, therefore, seems to us to be fostering articulation, helping teens to practice talking about their faith, providing practice at using vocabularies, grammars, stories, and key messages of faith. Our observation is that religious education in the United States is currently failing with youth when it comes to the articulation of faith.[6]

Recently during the church school hour a teacher related to me that she had just heard a beautiful prayer. It came from a seventeen-year-old girl who has been attending church for about five years. This teen became very active in church several years ago when she was given the opportunity to speak in church by reading the Scripture. She later became a member of the choir and started attending church school. Ironically, this teen has not been baptized but prays much better than many who have and are long-standing members of the congregation.

Teens who are given these opportunities often develop a sense of excitement about their churches and worship. No one wants to invest in something if they feel they and their gifts are not needed, not wanted.

The experience is spiritually nurturing by equipping teens to articulate their faith and have a deeper understanding and connection to their faith. "When teens engage in leading each other in a prayer of adoration, a time of confession, reading Scripture, or reading a blessing, they are learning the language of faith, and by doing so, they gain confidence in what they say they believe."[7]

When we mentor and prepare youth, we discover, sometimes surprisingly, that they learn to speak about their faith through reading, praying, singing, drama, dance, music, testimony, or participating in other ways. The experience often brings joy and affirmation. This involvement as a teen in worship frequently sparks an interest in other areas of the church and most importantly gives them the desire to participate in other worship services.

Mentoring youth is vitally important to faith formation. Through these experiences, youth leaders can empower young people to live for Christ, preparing leaders to advance God's kingdom in the world. It also provides a tremendous blessing to the community of believers.

I recall one Sunday morning sitting in the pulpit, waiting to preach. The choir prepared to sing, and I heard a beautiful male voice singing, "Hush Somebody's Calling My Name." I looked back at the choir, and it was our son singing. He was animated and walking as he sang. I had no idea that he had that kind of a voice. The musician and choir director had been mentoring him for months without my knowledge, and now that teen is a chaplain in the Air Force, serving presently in South Korea.

Worship, Music, and Faith Formation

Recently, I was in conversation with a group of Black youth, and I heard them say, "The church needs to be more modern." I pressed them to help me understand what they meant by "more modern." What came out of the dialogue was mainly about music as they referred to singing out of hymnals. The conversation reminded me of when I pastored in one small town, and when I would tell Black people

I was the pastor there, they would all respond, "That is the place where they sing out of hymnals."

Growing up in Barrs Chapel CME Church in rural northwest Tennessee, one would sing what trained musicians felt was church music, that is, mainly hymns. Occasionally, other sheet music was used, but my faith formation was aided greatly by hearing and singing the hymns. When I was in seminary, I discovered that not all hymns were written in the eighteenth and nineteenth centuries. I was introduced through new hymnals to "very modern" hymns. The definition of "very modern" was it had words that I understood and related to me.

I have come to appreciate teens, emerging adults, and young adults who want music that is relatable to their experiences. I now believe I understand the teens' definition of "more modern." Our focus groups affirm that music is an integral part of worship; therefore, it needs to be presented in a language that the youth can hear.

At one of the other churches I pastored, we hired a new musician who was to play for all choirs, including the youth choir. The musician became frustrated and suddenly left the church. He later said it was because the youth could not appreciate real music. Of course, the music he was trying to get them to sing was the music of his liking, and truthfully, it did not even speak to the baby boomers.

In Black churches, a youth choir is often in operation. It is not anything new. There is newer or "more modern" music that fits well with youth but may be challenging to baby boomers. I believe this is one of the characteristics of the Black church I speak about in Chapter 6, adaptability and change. The bottom line is that local Black churches must meet the challenges of "more modern," that is, music for Black adolescents. Perhaps Christian education directors might engage a youth or youths to teach adults about lyrics from modern music.

Another set of words emerged from the dialogue with this group of youth. They said that worship needs to be more engaging for youth. One of the youth said "fun," and another said "entertaining." It is interesting how a worship service can be both these things for adults but not for youth. The youth in this group went on to talk about the worship not connecting.

I say in *Faith Formation of a People*,

> Worship meets our essential needs, which include community and connectedness, solitude, and healing. Additionally, it provides a space where we are called to something meaningful, where we are transformed, where we can practice faithfulness. It is more than a rote form. Rather it can give a breakthrough of healing to a grieving heart. It can break the chain and illuminate a muddled mind. It can transform a bunch of mixed-up individuals into a community of believers.[8]

It seems from my experience that part of the community sometimes feels worship should be quiet and subdued and another group feels it is to be moving and noisy. The truth of the matter is that both groups may have it right. One of the missing ingredients is dialogue.

Perhaps a way to bridge the gap and to build community is to create intergenerational ministry. Generally speaking, intergenerational ministry can be defined as ministry that involves and incorporates the entire church, from each individual to the church community, so as to nurture spiritual growth and maturity mutually. Research noted the importance of relationships with the church body and parents as an important factor for teenagers remaining in the church after youth group. This coincides with what I write about Black church and family in Chapter 6.

Intergenerational ministry may curb the "us against them" syndrome. The youth I engaged in dialogue wanted change to take place now. They were convinced through their statements that my generation is too old to relate to what they are expressing. And the pervading issue was that tradition gets in the way of change. When I hear youth wanting worship their own way, I often hear a frustration that others always get their preferred worship style but the youth never get theirs. For me, the prescription for this is love. When I love someone, I want what's best for them. I want them to have what they need. Love helps me want for the other person a worship experience that is what they need.

I often hear youth use "allow" language referring to what adults do with youth in the church. For me, the church is just as much theirs (the youth), and the language of "allowing" reflects a sense of ownership on the part of grown-ups that might be what is but not what should be. Worship is often seen as "belonging" to the middle and older adults—"they've invested so much"—almost like shareholders with a greater number of votes. Wouldn't it be amazing if those middle and older adults understood that the church is theirs to tend until they give it away to the next generation?

Passionate Worship

The regular practice of worship gives people an interpretive lens, helping us see the world through God's eyes. Among the many competing interpretive contexts in which people are immersed—fierce individualism, acquisitive consumerism, intense nationalism, political partisanship, hopeless negativism, naïve optimism—worship helps people perceive themselves, their world, their relationships, and their responsibilities in ways that include God's revelation in Christ. The language of the Spirit—love, grace, joy, hope, forgiveness, compassion, justice, community—provides the means to express interior experience and relational aspirations. Stories of faith—Scripture, parable, testimony—deepen perception and meaning. The practices of worship—singing, praying, the sacraments—rehearse connection to God and to others. People look at the world in a different way and rehearse their unique calling as people of God and their identity as the body of Christ. Worship changes the way people experience their whole lives.

Ethnographic research supports that Black adolescents desire passionate worship. The work of Robert Schnase, a United Methodist bishop, has been helpful in giving clarity to what we heard from those to whom we listened.

When I hear young people talk about tradition, I get the sense they are talking about dry, routine, boring, and predictable. It is the same format Sunday after Sunday but has no spirit or zest to it. I hear from young people's need for passionate worship their desire to discard tradition, but in reality, I think they mean traditionalism. I don't hear it as a discard of all aspects of worship, but to change the approach. What I hear is not a need for worship to be in a certain venue or with a particular style of dress, but for worship to be authentic and passionate. The intense desire for authenticity and passion that typically characterizes adolescence can be fed through the kind of worship I hear them calling for. This type of worship is enlivening for adults, too, who have sometimes allowed themselves to be lulled into a sense of complacency and routine. For adolescents, the complementary disdain for hypocrisy is triggered by inauthentic, Spirit-less worship. In short, passionate worship connects with the passion adolescents feel naturally. Schnase puts it this way:

> Passionate Worship can be highly formal, with robes, acolytes, stained glass, organ music, orchestral accompaniment, and hardwood pews with hymnals on the rack in front. Or Passionate Worship can take place in an auditorium, gym, public park, or storefront, with casually dressed leaders, videos projected on screens, folding chairs, and the supporting beat of percussion, keyboard, and bass guitar. Authentic, compelling worship derives from the experience of God's presence, the desire of worshippers for God's word, and the changed heart that people deliberately seek when they gather in the presence of other Christians. An hour of Passionate Worship changes all the other hours of the week.[9]

However, when young people experience worship in one formal way consistently, it becomes traditional. It becomes too predictable and oftentimes is done routinely as an obligation and without joy. It is disconnected from their lived experience. It is therefore without passion. Black youth desire to worship with a passion that allows for freedom to "flip the script." This is contagious. I have noticed when this freedom is given, more and more youth participate who otherwise are passive in worship.

When congregations are not open to new or "more modern" forms of worship that young people offer (e.g., dance and mime), young people feel ignored, not heard, and not valued. Worship is a place where youth can and should be involved. As mentioned earlier, there is a need for mentorship, but as I mention here, there is a need also to listen to youth.

So, what is passionate worship? I believe Schnase gives a useful and helpful description:

> Passionate Worship fosters a yearning to authentically honor God with excellence and with an unusual clarity about connecting people to God. Whether fifteen hundred people attend, or fifteen, Passionate Worship is alive, authentic, fresh, and engaging. People are honest before God and open to God's presence, truth, and will. People so desire such worship that they reorder their lives to belong. The empty places in their souls are filled. They experience a compelling sense of belonging to the body of Christ.[10]

I hear Black adolescents putting emphasis on "real" or authentic honoring of God. This means being listened to by adults and given opportunities to plan, lead, and participate in worship. It also means making love an action word that connects all people. When this occurs, the empty spaces mentioned by Schnase are filled with God's love and grace. It seems to me this is what worship should do. It is pointed to

God, but we as participants benefit as the worship connects us as a community of faith.

Worship should express our devotion, our honor and love of God. *Passionate* describes an intense desire, an ardent spirit, strong feelings, and a sense of heightened importance. Passionate speaks of an emotional connection that goes beyond intellectual consent.[11] One of the obligations of Christian educators is to provide avenues of learning for the entire congregation to know what is going on in worship. I think the more we know about passionate worship, the less apathetic we become. The more educated we become about worship, the more passionate we become toward worship. Black youth are nurtured into a relationship with God through prayers, liturgy, songs, and sermons. Additionally, they are formed through their participation, which is why it is critical that youth are included in all aspects of worship, including the planning.

Insufficient planning by leaders, apathy, lack of education about worship, poor quality music, and unkempt facilities contribute to an experience that people approach with a sense of obligation rather than joy. Worship loses its passion.

Interpersonal conflict can also threaten the worship life of community, with participants and leaders distracted and exhausted by antagonism. Some services feel inauthentic or self-indulgent as leaders push themselves into the center of attention. Some leaders of worship spend an overabundance of time at the microphone saying repetitive phrases, such as, "Give the Lord a hand clap of praise," that irritate and distract those attempting to worship.

Or services can seem as somber as a funeral when people attend out of obligation, respect, or genuine affection, but privately they wish they were somewhere else. Services sometimes include so many announcements, jokes, digressions, and stories that have nothing to do with the theme that it feels like a loosely planned, poorly led public meeting. Even with worship in homes, dinner churches, or online communities, conversation can degenerate into complaining or rumor mongering. Worship may be the first contact people have with a faith community, and yet guests may not find genuine warmth or a compelling message. When this happens, people come and go without experiencing God.

Passionate worship causes congregations to be spiritually alive, and spiritually alive congregations practice passionate worship. Out of this comes a strong sense of expectancy, vibrancy, and curiosity about how God's presence will become known during worship. It seems to me that spiritually alive churches foster enthusiasm that is seen in the musicians, worship leaders, ushers, and officers of the church. People arrive early for worship in anticipation of an encounter and experience with God. The church is kept immaculate. There is a spirit of unity among the worshippers and a welcoming spirit for those who don't normally attend.

On Sunday morning, leaders and worshipers expect something significant to take place, and they're eager to be part of it. They expect God to be present and to speak to them a word of forgiveness, hope, or direction. Singing together, joining in prayer, listening to the Word, confessing sins, celebrating the sacraments—through these simple acts, they intermingle their lives with one another and with God. Worship is compelling. It permeates the air.

As a pastor, I have become more and more aware that engaging youth in worship requires intentionality. Although this century has different circumstances, I believe reflection on my own youth experience is helpful and creates empathy. As adult leaders in the church, we must look for and intentionally create opportunities for youth engagement that assumes the experiences of youth as the norm. It starts with what we often neglect to do: listening to youth and taking action when possible. Listening also includes educating and equipping youth, especially theologically. As adults, we must address the why questions often before they are asked. In short, we need to begin by challenging ourselves to assume that youth are the church today, that the church is theirs as much as it is ours as adults.

Exercise: Plan a worship service designed specifically for Black adolescents. Plan it with them or help them plan it themselves.

NOTES

1. The foundation of this research is a series of focus groups with young adults who are engaged in African American congregations presently and were engaged in them as adolescents. Approximately sixty youth participated in eight focus group sessions conducted by this book's coauthors from 2018 to 2020. The focus groups were conducted following appropriate human subjects protocols to ensure ethical and safe research. The goal of the focus groups was to hear the witness of those who were recently adolescents in the Black church about the things that sustained them about that involvement and kept them involved as young adults. Focus group questions were designed to give participants the opportunity to tell the stories of their experiences as an adolescent in the Black church and to reflect on those experiences.

2. Sharon Vellema, "Teens, Worship, and Faith Formation," September 10, 2013, Calvin Institute of Christian Worship, https://worship.calvin.edu/resources/resource-library/teens-worship-and-faith-formation/.

3. Robert Keeley, ed., *Shaped by God: Twelve Essentials for Nurturing Faith in Children, Youth, and Adults* (Grand Rapids, MI: Faith Alive Christian Resources, 2010), 72.

4. Marjorie Lindner Gunnoe and Claudia DeVries Beversluis, "Youth, Worship, and Faith Formation: Findings from a National Survey," Reformed Worship, https://www.reformedworship.org/article/march-2009/youth-worship-and-faith-formation.

5. John H. Westerhoff III, *Will Our Children Have Faith?* (New York: Seabury Press, 1976), 56.

6. Melinda Denton and Christian Smith, *Soul Searching: The Religious and Spiritual Lives of American Teenagers* (New York: Oxford University Press, 2005), 267–68.

7. Vellema.

8. Carmichael Crutchfield, *The Formation of a People: Christian Education and the African American Church* (Valley Forge, PA: Judson Press, 2020), 80.

9. Robert Schnase, *Five Practices of Fruitful Congregations* (Nashville: Abingdon, 2018), 53.

10. Ibid.

11. Ibid.

Chapter 5

Faith Formation in the Midst of a Violent World

"Young Black men and teens are killed by guns twenty times more than their white counterparts, CDC data shows."[1] This was the headline of an article in *USA Today* on February 25, 2021. Countless children and youth are exposed to gun violence each year—at home, at school, in their communities, or through the media. Black youth who live in an atmosphere of violence within their own neighborhoods and homes, and who witness a steady diet of violence through television, movies, and video or online gaming do not possess the ability to separate the types of violence when they emerge into the real world. Because, on television, the taking of a life poses no particular problems, they equate this response to their own lives and thus do not consider the consequences of their actions prior to taking up a weapon in real life and using it.[2]

The problem goes even deeper than this. In the story shared in Chapter 2, a shift was identified that has taken place in the last few decades from a standard of fighting it out (meaning fists and words) to shooting it out. The introduction of weapons (knives and guns of increasing deadliness) into disagreements that used to be arbitrated with fists and words has escalated the level of violence to the point that those who feel threatened expect they must obtain increasing firepower just to defend themselves. This kind of firepower in the hands of adolescents (and children) whose brains have not yet fully mastered impulse control creates a situation fraught with danger.

What Were They Thinking . . . ?

In *Secrets of the Teenage Brain*, Sheryl G. Feinstein explains how brain development plays into violence concerning adolescents. She states that violence and aggression increase during the teenage years, particularly for males.[3] She points out that environment plays a role, but adds that the brain also plays a role.[4] She goes on to explain how serotonin levels have been linked to aggression and violence. Unfortunately for the adolescent, levels of serotonin in the prefrontal cortex are especially low, reducing its ability to control the emotional amygdala. There are also lower levels of glucose metabolism, an energy source, in the mus, and other emotional areas of the brain. As a result, we find less energy in the decision-making, logical part of the brain and more and more energy in the emotional areas of the brain. Not the balances needed for healthy choices.[5]

In our focus groups, answers to "What do you think about when you hear that someone has been the victim of violence?" were varied. There was no consensus even within specific focus groups. However, consistent in the answers was either disgust about it or desensitization to it.

During one focus group, some of the participants became very emotional. Three of the members of that group had just lost a friend from the church choir to gun violence. They said that they asked God why questions out of their anger. They also were hurt and wanted justice to take place. This led to the question in the sense of helplessness: What can we do about it? This story raised the question surrounding the code of silence. Practiced by some Blacks, this code of silence is often reported by law enforcement agencies as a reason for many unsolved murder cases.

Some of those in focus groups reported that they try not to think about all the violence. Some of their statements reminded me of a conversation I once had with a young male clergy colleague who lived at the time in Atlanta, Georgia. He told me that gunshots sounded in his neighborhood every day, and he had come to the point where he did not really hear them any longer. Contemporary issues of gun violence continue to escalate to the point where people think it is just part of living in America. It's almost as though our culture is not hearing it anymore. When I asked one group of young men what the church was saying about gun violence, there was a silence in the room in general. When group members broke through to talk, they spoke about how individuals were talking about it as an issue, but they could not say it was the overall church's voice. They could not identify that the church as an entity had spoken about gun violence or did anything to address it as a group. For a church that claims to follow the model of Jesus, there seems to be radio silence on this major issue of oppression and injustice that affects church and culture alike.

How can or does the Black church address the issue of gun violence in America? And how is the church addressing gun violence as it relates to Black adolescents? We see one response to these questions from a group of Black clergy in Philadelphia. There the Black Clergy of Philadelphia and Vicinity laid out a multifaceted plan to combat the gun violence plaguing the city. Rev. Gregory Holston, chairman of the Criminal Justice Reform and Violence Prevention Committee for the clergy group, said about gun violence, "It's spreading to our children and our young people who are picking up the habits and the culture and the anger and the hostility that is happening in their own community, and they are picking it up and spreading it, one to another."[6] He goes on: "We have to intervene early in their lives to be able to make sure that we stop the spread of this virus [of violence]. Those who are engaged in this violence right now, we need to do things to restore them, to transform them, to change their lives and give them hope and so much of the murder and the destruction is coming from a sense of hopelessness, and it's up to us to give our children the hope that they need."[7]

The challenge for the Black church is to find ways to affect the lives of adolescents as early as possible with measures that make a difference. I am not proposing a new program for the church per se; however, I do argue that the Black church has opportunities to impact neighborhoods. It is my contention that the road to faith formation of adolescents in the Black church begins by naming the issue of gun violence as something to which our faith compels us to respond. Step two is paying more attention to our neighborhoods.

Jack Seymour, emeritus professor of religious education at Garrett-Evangelical Theological Seminary, states in *Educating for Redemptive Community* that many social problems can be traced directly to inequality—poor educational attainment, poor health, increasingly inadequate neighborhoods, limiting of resources for schools and preschools, and crime.[8]

The latest maps of coronavirus cases in the United States confirm much of what we already know about the economics of location: People in poor neighborhoods have it worse. Health care isn't as accessible, the ability to socially distance is less, and many residents fall into the role of essential workers, unable to work from home. What new research shows is that the number of poor neighborhoods in metropolitan areas has doubled from 1980—and most existing low-income areas only fell deeper into poverty.[9]

In addition to the violence within their communities, Black adolescents face the constant danger or possibility of being brutalized or killed by law enforcement, facing violence at the hands of those who are sworn to serve and protect all people. Two separate occasions come to mind personally when I think about racial profiling or being signaled out as a Black teenager. Both situations took place in small cities in the southern region of the United States. One incident occurred during my sophomore year in college. I was driving a nice car, a Volkswagen, that I had borrowed from my older brother. Three times in a span of two or three hours I was pulled over by police for no apparent reason. The explanation given to me the third time was that a robbery had occurred, and the robber was driving a car that fit the description of the car I was driving. Even today I still tremble when I hear police sirens and see lights in my rearview mirror, as I have a persistent image of a white man with a gun shining a flashlight throughout the window of the car I am driving.

When I was twenty years old, I was riding with my fraternity brothers and the driver stopped to get a soft drink from a vending machine outside a small convenience store. The machine took the money but did not dispense a beverage. My fraternity brother knocked on the door of the store where the attendant had just locked the door and was standing, visible, inside. Within minutes three or four patrol cars pulled in behind our car, and officers came out with guns pointed. Again, one of the policemen, with a gun in one hand and a flashlight in the other, ordered us to get in a line with police cars in front and back of our car as we drove to the police station. They took our driver to the back of the police station and made us sit where we could not see him. We sat there for what seemed to be an eternity. They were charging our driver with driving a stolen vehicle, although it was loaned to him by his sister.

And, lest we think this was all "way back when," as I write this chapter (April 2021), a twenty-year-old Black man named Daunte Wright was shot to death in Minnesota. The record reports that he was pulled over for having an expired tag. He called his mother and was ordered to get out of the car and hang up the phone. In a matter of minutes, he was shot and killed by the police officer, who claimed she had mistaken her gun for her taser.

What does all of this have to do with faith formation of Black adolescents? It is my argument that to make a difference we must enable the church to relate to and communicate with Black adolescents in their neighborhoods. If the church does not see these young women and men as their own sisters and brothers—their neighbors, as in the story Jesus told in response to a lawyer's question asking for a definition of who exactly constituted a neighbor to whom he was responsible. Jesus' response was to tell the story about a person of another country traveling a dangerous road who responded to the need of a man left for dead by robbers (Luke 10:25-37). This person who had no reason to know Jewish law did what a good human being would do—he helped a person he found who was in need. Those who should have known what God wanted them to do in such a situation failed to do so. At the end of the story, Jesus asked the lawyer to apply what he heard in the story: "Which of these three, do you think, was a neighbor to the man who fell into the hands of robbers?" The lawyer responded, "The one who showed him mercy." The story concludes with Jesus' statement: "Go and do likewise" (Luke 10:36-37). The church doesn't have to decide whether those who live around them are worthy. The point of Jesus' story was that "showing mercy" is the mark of one who is a neighbor. The church must show mercy to those around them—including the Black adolescents in their neighborhoods. Being a neighbor is the beginning step but not the final step. Equipping ourselves with tools to understand and be good neighbors to the Black adolescents in our communities requires tools. These tools include the use of critical consciousness, the use of the transformation model of education, and emphasis of emancipatory hope. I will elaborate on these tools later in this chapter.

Several years ago, as part of a youth ministry, I taught at the seminary a class named "Working with Black Youth." I engaged the students several weeks into listening to, reading the lyrics, and theologizing about rap music. Tupac Shakur's music was one we analyzed. Recently in a contemplative pedagogy class at the church, I again invited adults to think deeply about the words of a particular song of Shakur. Here are some of the lyrics from the song "Dear Mama" that I believe speak volumes about what was going on with this particular young man.

We was poorer than the other little kids
And even though we had different daddies, the same drama
When things went wrong we'd blame mama
I reminisce on the stress I caused, it was hell
Huggin' on my mama from a jail cell
And who'd think in elementary, hey
I'd see the penitentiary one day?
    And running from the police, that's right
Mama catch me, put a whoopin' to my backside
And even as a crack fiend, mama

You always was a Black queen, mama
I finally understand
For a woman it ain't easy trying to raise a man.[10]

Equipping Black Adolescents Means Shifting Our Faith Formation

First, we must acknowledge that our neighborhoods are in desperate need of transformation and social reform. I think without a doubt that our public schools are one of the means to make this happen. It is my argument that this will happen only as we empower our people through an educational process that discards the banking concept[11] of education in favor of a problem-posing concept[12] and as we desocialize using critical consciousness.[13] Most of us were raised in educational systems that told us what to think (banking) rather than giving us tools to critically analyze problems (critical consciousness) and dialogue toward addressing them (problem-posing education). There is power in human agency. Students are not the objects but the subjects in education who can make a powerful impact in transformation and social reform.

Some fundamental and related questions must be addressed for which these tools will be helpful. Why does it seem that African American men have so little regard for the lives of other Black men? Why would they place a higher value on material possessions than on human life? And do these young men reflect hatred for their community and love of wealth? R. L'Heureux Lewis-McCoy, a professor of sociology and Black studies at the City College of New York, says, "Given the high levels of segregation that many Black males grow up in, the decreased employment opportunities, long term unemployment, and failing schools, the chances for young Black males to develop a sense of healthy self-worth are limited. Instead, material possessions and contestation over space like [street] corners can be the spaces where worth and value are determined."[14] Lewis-McCoy challenges us to think about where these young men derive their values. "Black males, we cannot forget, are members of an American society which glorifies material wealth," he said. "But they are some of society's members with the fewest routes available to gain that wealth without putting their own and others' lives in danger."[15]

Eddie Glaude Jr., a professor of religion and African American studies at Princeton University, echoed this sentiment by emphasizing the need to broaden our understanding of victimization. "This is a horrible act. But we must try to understand the context that produced it," Glaude said. "It isn't simply that these young Black men are evil. In so many ways, we have failed them. I am not absolving them of their responsibility for the crime. I am simply holding us responsible for the world that produced them."[16]

Onlookers may find it easy to blame our young Black brothers and sisters for their misdeeds, dismissing them as evil because of the violent strategies they choose. However, it seems to me that the truer and more complex place to start that addresses the root issues is that we have failed many of our adolescents, male and female. We have failed them as neighbors in the way Jesus used the title. One of the most egregious ways we have failed to be neighbors to the young people in our communities is around education, when we allow banking models of education to keep them anesthetized rather than engaging them as valued human beings who have something to contribute, both to their own situations and to the larger community.

Critical Consciousness
Contemporary research has found that critical consciousness not only expands young people's commitment to challenging pervasive injustice,[17] but also increases academic achievement and engagement.[18] In particular, school-based programming designed to foster critical consciousness has been shown to increase academic engagement and achievement[19] and enrollment in higher education.[20] In explaining these relationships, researchers have suggested that critical consciousness of oppressive social forces can replace feelings of isolation and self-blame for one's challenges with a sense of engagement in a broader collective

struggle for social justice.[21] Research also suggests that a critical consciousness about racism, specifically, can motivate Black students to resist oppressive forces through persisting in school and achieving in academics.[22] This motivation is often fueled by a desire to prove wrong the stereotypes embedded in racist structures and institutions.[23]

In *The Formation of a People,* I contend that education has been engrossed and immersed in a transmission model or banking concept of education. I describe this model as the teacher who becomes the subject (expert), the one with the knowledge who pours or deposits into the student who, in turn, becomes the object of all the knowledge she or he needs to know. At some point, maybe at midterm, the student withdraws the knowledge he or she has stored and places it on a test.[24] In the church an example of the transmission model is when teachers insist and practice with children to memorize the books of the Bible as they appear and then expect them to recite that during a worship service or other time to display their abilities. Although this may have some educational value, it has no formational or transformational value of its own. From my experience of more than twenty-five years of education, the test often ends the process. In this transmission model, students, or members of churches, don't gain the ability to draw connections between what the teacher is saying and their own lives. Also, in the transmission model, students have questions that go unanswered because most of the communication is planned and prescribed, which ignores the learners' needs within the classroom. Communication flows in one direction. Students who learn best in other ways or who have obstacles in their learning process are left without options in this model. Another type of student in this transmission model sees the teacher placing emphasis on planting and germinating knowledge that eventually leads to that knowledge sprouting up in the learner. This is to say a concept is provided to the student (planting), and over a period of time (a term), the student comes to know the concept but easily dismisses the information after it is used on a test. During most of my student life, I experienced this model of education.[25]

The Transformational Model of Education

In contrast is the transformation model. The transformative model of education or pedagogy is critical pedagogy. With this model, the learner gets out into the real world and participates in real activities; thus, he or she gains realistic pictures to visualize and experience. The communication freely flows from learner to learner, and the teacher becomes a partner in the learning process.[26] This model starts with the lived experience of learners who build on the knowledge they already have with layers of new insights, understandings, and connections. Evidence of learning in this model can be experienced as a change in the learners' own actions. An example of other signs of learning might be that learners use their new understandings to influence others and bring about social change and transformation.

So, what will it take to change our educational processes so that Black adolescents can be more committed to social reform and transformation? I am given encouragement and hope by the writings of Ira Shor. Shor offers the concept of desocialization or to let go in two areas. (1) Desocialization (let go) from traditional school conditioning that interferes with critical thought. (2) Desocialization (let go) from mass culture, from regressive values, such as racism, sexism, classism, homophobia, self-reliant individualism, excessive consumerism, and so on. He goes on to offer a model for desocialization called critical consciousness. Shor defines the three-step model of development leading to critical consciousness that was formulated by Paulo Freire: intransitive, semi-transitive, and critical transitive thought. The intransitive level is where people deny the power they have to change their lives and society. At the semi-transitive level, people see life as unrelated parts and believe change can come only one thing at a time. In critical transitive thought, people make broad connections between individual experience and social issues, between single problems and larger social systems. Movements begin at this level. What will it take to change our educational processes? Perhaps it requires that we ourselves experience critical consciousness at the third level, recognizing in our individual experiences the broad connections between single problems and larger social systems. If we make this connection, we can see that our experiences can inform our actions, and our actions alongside the actions of others can bring about change for the adolescents who are our neighbors. We can begin to see the steps to change and work together to make change happen.

Case in Point: Voting by African American Young Adults in Recent Presidential Elections

A brief analysis of the United States presidential elections during the twenty-first century is helpful in looking at these three levels of critical consciousness. An article in the *Commercial Appeal*, a Memphis, Tennessee, newspaper, provides experiences of Black young adults engaged in the voting process.[27] Abigail Barge of Memphis, Tennessee, says she did not vote in the 2016 election because she didn't think she was educated enough at the time. She states that she voted in the 2020 election primary for Elizabeth Warren in the Democratic primary. When asked what made the difference, she said, "After everything that happened under the Trump administration, I regretted the decision of 2016. I decided this time I was going to do my homework and actually go vote."

She went on to say in 2016 she didn't want to do the wrong thing because she wasn't sure about who to vote for, "but now, I decided that I wanted to do something because even if the result doesn't turn out favorable to me, I can at least say I did my part." It seems that Abigail has moved to the third level of critical consciousness, that is, transitive thought. She has the mind to change things by doing her part.

Then there was Grant Posey, who voted for the first time at the age of twenty-five. He says that health care drove him to the polls in the March 2020 primary election to vote for Bernie Sanders. He had done his homework and noted that Sanders had been consistent for decades on his position on health care. It seems that Grant was also in the third level of critical consciousness. He came to the point of seeing through the lenses of hope.

While young people typically don't turn out to vote in large numbers, they did turn out in respectable numbers during the Tennessee Democratic primary in 2008, when Barack Obama was on the ballot. Voters aged seventeen to twenty-nine increased their share of the electorate to 13 percent—6 percent higher than in 2004. Nationally, Black voters in that age range made up 18 percent of the voters in 2008 and 19 percent in 2012. So, what is it that made a difference? Why can't any of the Democratic candidates motivate youth turnout in the same way that Obama did more than a decade ago? Perhaps the answer revolves around one word: Hope.

Obama's catchphrase was "hope and change." He was an example of what hope meant for many young people—an African American man who overcame setbacks to become the editor of *Harvard Law Review* and dared to defy expectations to become the nation's first African American president. Unlike Donald Trump, Obama focused his energies on trying to solve big problems, such as fixing a health care system that leads too many Americans into debt and death, and not on scapegoating immigrants and seeing people as problems. Yet much of what Trump did was to gin up fear, and many young people don't respond to fear as much as they do to hope.

Critical consciousness is at the root of effective faith formation, and effective faith formation is fueled by hope—the hope of a more loving and just world to which God calls us.

Emancipatory Hope

Faith formation of Black adolescents hinges on hope. Evelyn Parker names it as emancipatory hope and defines it as the expectation that the issues of hegemonic relations—race, class, and gender dominance—will be toppled. To have emancipatory hope is acknowledging one's personal agency in God's vision for human equality.[28] Parker writes that verbs such as "challenge," "examine," "confront," "free," and "transform" are commonly used in association with emancipatory hope.[29] Fannie Lou Hamer as an exemplar of emancipatory hope. Parker points out the work of Hamer that includes being a freedom fighter for all of humankind as a worker of civil rights activism from the early 1950s until her death in 1977.[30]

Furthermore, Parker helps us see two critical aspects of faith formation in Black adolescents: epistemology and spirituality. Parker points out that the process of meaning-making in Black adolescents is sabotaged by the ideological hegemony of racism, sexism, and classism. Black youth must find ways to subvert these oppressive forms of ideology.[31] Ministry with Black youth must free them from the ideology that demands conformity, that stratifies and classifies standards set by dominant culture. Ministry focusing upon emancipatory hope fosters thought and consciousness that is imaginative, creative, and critical.[32] Faith formation of Black youth based upon emancipatory hope fosters new ways of meaning-making for Black youth victimized by an oppressive dominant culture. Youth set free by emancipatory hope envision an alternative world free of "political, economic, racial and cultural injustice."[33]

"Emancipatory hope also fosters a potent spirituality in African American adolescents," writes Parker.[34] This helps adolescents to reflect critically on injustice and sharpens their coping skills. Spirituality always fortifies adolescents and assures them that God is present. Parker says, "Such spirituality gives testimony to the presence of the 'triune God.'"[35] Parker states that this is illustrated in the life of Fannie Lou Hamer and the biblical witness of the story of Joseph found in Genesis.[36]

Conclusion

Violence, and particularly gun violence, is a reality in America. It affects the lives of Black teens as they navigate being adolescents. The Black church has historically provided a means of liberation. In the twenty-first century the Black church is challenged to provide transformative ministry to adolescents, both within and outside the church, that is relevant to their lives and equips them to bring about social change.

The Black church must move beyond providing educational ministry that transmits only knowledge, shifting instead to more effectively transforming lives. This involves a focus on emancipatory hope and critical consciousness, providing education for communities to survive and thrive as adolescents find and discover their self-identity. It is teaching in a way that brings new life to a people. In short, the Black church is challenged to live the hope we have in God as we engage with our neighbors.

Question: Explain the importance of self-identity and the impact it has on faith formation.

NOTES

1. Naada Hassanien, "Young Black Men and Teens Are Killed by Guns 20 Times More Than Their White Counterparts, CDC Data Shows," February 25, 2021, *USA Today*, usatoday.com/story/news/health/2021/02/23/young-Black-men-teens-made-up-more-than-third-2019-gun-homicides/4559929001/.

2. Roger D. Turner, in *Black on Black Violence: Moving Towards Realistic Explanations and Solutions in Black on Black Crime*, ed. P. Ray Kedia (Bristol, IN: Wyndham Hall Press, 1994), 6.

3. Sheryl Feinstein, *Secrets of the Teenage Brain: Research-Based Strategies for Reaching and Teaching Today's Adolescents* (Thousand Oaks, CA: Corwin, 2009), 123.

4. Ibid.

5. Ibid.

6. Ayana Jones, "Black Clergy Group Unveils Plan to Address Gun Violence in Philadelphia," March 19, 2021, *Philadelphia Tribune*, on WHYY website, https://whyy.org/articles/Black-clergy-group-unveils-plan-to-address-gun-violence-in-philadelphia/.

7. Ibid.

8. Denise Janssen, ed., *Educating for Redemptive Community: Essays in Honor of Jack Seymour and Margaret Ann Crain* (Eugene, OR: Wipf & Stock, 2015), 15.

9. Marie Patino, "Poor Neighborhoods Are Only Getting Poorer," May 26, 2020, Bloomberg CityLab, https://www.bloomberg.com/news/articles/2020-05-26/poor-neighborhoods-fall-deeper-into-poverty.

10. "Dear Mama" lyrics by 2Pac, https://www.lyrics.com/lyric/2526916/2Pac/Dear+Mama.

11. "Education thus becomes an act of depositing, in which the students are the depositories and the teacher is the depositor. Instead of communicating, the teacher issues communiques and makes deposits which the students patiently receive, memorize, and repeat. This is the 'banking' concept of education, in which the scope of action allowed to the students extends only as far as receiving, filing, and storing the deposits. They do, it is true, have the opportunity to become col-

lectors or cataloguers of the things they store. But in the last analysis, it is the people themselves who are filed away through the lack of creativity, transformation, and knowledge in this (at best) misguided system. For apart from inquiry, apart from the praxis, individuals cannot be truly human. Knowledge emerges only through invention and re-invention, through the restless, impatient, continuing, hopeful inquiry human beings pursue in the world, with the world, and with each other.

"In the banking concept of education, knowledge is a gift bestowed by those who consider themselves knowledgeable upon those whom they consider to know nothing. Projecting an absolute ignorance onto others, a characteristic of the ideology of oppression, negates education and knowledge as processes of inquiry. The teacher presents himself to his students as their necessary opposite; by considering their ignorance absolute, he justifies his own existence. The students, alienated like the slave in the Hegelian dialectic, accept their ignorance as justifying the teacher's existence—but, unlike the slave, they never discover that they educate the teacher." Paulo Freire, "The 'Banking' Concept of Education," http://puente2014.pbworks.com/w/file/fetch/87465079/freire_banking_concept.pdf.

12. "The 'problem posing' education model is basically a method of education that encourages students to not only engage in discussions with their teachers, but also question the information that they obtain in their classes. It is a system that dissuades them from simply listening in class and memorizing key facts for their next assignments, thereby promoting both critical thinking and learning for the sake of improving one's knowledge. According to Freire, it is the exact opposite of 'banking education,' which discourages active participation in classes." "Problem Posing Education Model," https://www.bartleby.com/essay/Problem-Posing Education Model FC9ZJY496V.

13. "Brazilian educator Paulo Freire (1970) conceived of critical consciousness while working with adult laborers in Brazil. Freire realized that inequality is sustained when the people most affected by it are unable to decode their social conditions. Freire proposed a cycle of critical consciousness development that involved gaining knowledge about the systems and structures that create and sustain inequity (critical analysis), developing a sense of power or capability (sense of agency), and ultimately committing to take action against oppressive conditions (critical action)." Aaliyah El-Amin, Scott Seider, Daren Graves, Jalene Tamerat, Shelby Clark, Madora Soutter, Jamie Johannsen, and Saira Malhotra, "Critical Consciousness: A Key to Student Achievement," February 4, 2017, Phi Delta Kappan, https://kappanonline.org/critical-consciousness-key-student-achievement/.

14. Rahiel Tesfamariam, "Understanding the Root Causes of Black-on-Black Violence," December 23, 2012, Washington Post, https://www.washingtonpost.com/blogs/therootdc/post/understanding-the-root-causes-of-Black-on-Black-violence/2012/12/03/d3609342-3d61-11e2-a2d9-822f58ac9fd5_blog.html.

15. Ibid.

16. Ibid.

17. Shawn Ginwright, Black Youth Rising: Activism and Racial Healing in Urban America (New York: Teachers College Press, 2010), 106ff; M. Diemer, A. Voight, and

R. Watts, "Critical Consciousness: Current Status and Future Directions," *New Directions for Child and Adolescent Development* 134 (2011): 43–57.

18. D. J. Carter, "Cultivating a Critical Race Consciousness for African-American School Success," *Educational Foundations* 22, no. 1-2 (2008): 11–28; C. O'Connor, "Dispositions Toward Collective Struggle and Educational Resilience in the Inner City: A Case Analysis of Six African-American High School Students," *American Educational Research Journal* 34, no. 4 (1997): 593–629.

19. N. Cabrera, O. Jaquette, R. Marx, and J. Milem, "Missing the (Student Achievement) Forest for All the (Political) Trees: Empiricism and the Mexican-American Studies Controversy in Tucson," *American Educational Research Journal* 51, no. 6 (2014): 1084–1118; J. Cammarota, "A Social Justice Approach to Achievement: Guiding Latina/o Students Toward Educational Attainment with a Challenging, Socially Relevant Curriculum," *Equity & Excellence in Education* 40, no. 1 (2007): 87–96; Thomas Dee and Emily Penner, "The Causal Effects of Cultural Relevance: Evidence from an Ethnic Studies Curriculum," CEPA Working Paper No. 16-01 (2016), Stanford Center for Education Policy Analysis, https://cepa.stanford.edu/sites/default/files/wp16-01-v201601.pdf.

20. J. Rogers and V. Terriquez, *Learning to Lead: The Impact of Youth Organizing on the Educational and Civic Trajectories of Low-Income Youth* (Los Angeles: Institute for Democracy, Education, and Access, 2013).

21. M. Diemer, L. Rapa, C. Park, and J. Perry, "Development and Validation of a Critical Consciousness Scale," *Youth & Society* (2014): 1–23; Ginwright.

22. Carter.

23. Carter; M. G. Sanders, "Overcoming Obstacles: Academic Achievement as a Response to Racism and Discrimination," *Journal of Negro Education* 66, no. 1 (1997): 83–93.

24. Carmichael Crutchfield, *The Formation of a People: Christian Education and the African American Church* (Valley Forge, PA: Judson Press, 2020), 125.

25. Ibid.

26. Ibid., 126.

27. Tonyaa Weathersbee, "Young People Must Vote Out of Hope for Their Future, Not Blind Hope in a Candidate," Memphis Commercial Appeal, March 5, 2020, https://www.commercialappeal.com/story/news/youth-voter-turnout-super-tuesday-memphis-tonyaa-weathersbee/4.

28. Evelyn L. Parker, *Trouble Don't Last Always: Emancipatory Hope among African American Adolescents* (Cleveland: Pilgrim Press, 2003), 11.

29. Ibid. 14.

30. Ibid., 17

31. Ibid., 20.

32. Ibid.

33. Ibid.

34. Ibid., 24.

35. Ibid., 22.

36. Ibid.

Chapter 6

The Church and the Black Family

A study of the Black family begins in Africa. "African families embody two contrasting bases for membership; consanguinity, which refers to kinship that is commonly presumed to be biologically based and conjugality that refers specifically to the affinal kinship created between spouses."[1] The African family structure, unlike the European structure, tends to form around consanguineal cores of adult siblings. The groups that form around these core members "include their spouses and children." When African people are married, they "tend not to go off and form new nuclear groupings but instead join an already existing compound of adjoining or contiguous dwellings composed of the extended family members."[2]

When Africans were taken from their homes and forced into slavery, they were separated from mothers, fathers, sisters, and brothers and were torn from extensive kinship networks. One of the most profound impacts of the transatlantic Middle Passage was the creation of a new family on the harrowing journey across the ocean. The transatlantic Middle Passage brought enslaved Africans to North and South America against their will over a several-hundred-year period in ships that had most of their passengers essentially stacked in the hull and chained to one another. During the months-long sojourn, most of the passengers never left these positions. Everything a human being does in a day took place in this position and location—which meant the hull became a horrifying and putrid mess. If you gave birth, it happened there with everyone looking on. If someone didn't survive, the body stayed where it was until some worker noticed and threw it overboard. People were typically chained together, and usually the low ceilings did not permit them to sit upright. The heat was intolerable, and the oxygen levels became so low that candles would not burn. Because crews feared insurrection, the Africans were allowed to go outside on the upper decks for only a few hours each day. Historians estimate that between 15 and 25 percent of the enslaved Africans bound for the Americas died aboard slave ships.[3] In the belly of the ship, family became whoever was shackled next to you. In the quest for survival, trusting one's neighbor became a critical strategy.

The Enslaved Experience in America

In some ways enslaved Black families very much resembled other families who lived in other times and places and under vastly different circumstances. Some husbands and wives loved each other; some did not get along. Children sometimes abided by parents' rules; other times they followed their own minds. Most parents loved their children and wanted to protect them. In some critical ways, though, the slavery that marked everything about their lives made these families very different. The following excerpt informs us:

> "I never knew a whole family to live together, till all were grown up, in my life," recalls Lewis Clarke of his twenty-five years enslaved in Kentucky. Families were separated due to sale, escape, early death from poor health, suicide, and murder by a slaveholder, overseer, slave patroller, or other dominant person. Separation also occurred within the plantation itself, e.g., by segregating "field slaves" from "house servants," removing children from parents to live together with a slave caretaker, or bringing children

fathered by the slaveholder to live in the "Big House."
How, then, did the slave family provide solace and
identity? "What the family does, and what the family
did for African Americans," writes historian Deborah
White Gray, "was create a world outside of the world
of work. It allowed for significant others. It allowed
a male slave to be more than just a brute beast. It allowed him to be a father, to be a son. It allowed
women to be mothers and to take on roles that were
outside of that of a slave, of a servant."[4]

Further, Jennifer Hallam writes,

As the plantation revolution swept across the South
in the late seventeenth and early eighteenth centuries
and the terms of racial slavery were concretized in law,
slaves found it increasingly difficult to form families.
Not only did the law forbid interracial wedlock and
deny Blacks legal rights to marry each other, but the
agricultural demands of Southern slave societies also
continued to generate a disproportionate population
of Black men in the colonies.[5]

"During nearly 250 years of slavery in the United States, enslaved
persons were frequently torn from their family members," Margaret
Crable writes. "Women were separated from their children on the auc-
tion block. Men and women could be sold from one plantation to another." What is more, "'The entire structure of slavery supported
the separation and the ongoing fragility of the Black family,' says Alisa
Morgan, assistant professor of history at the USC Dornsife College of
Letters, Arts and Sciences."[6]

However, slavery affected more than the family structure. Henry H.
Mitchell points out that slavery also struck a terrible blow to the
African worldview and value systems.[7] That said, I believe that the

African influence has continued in spite of slavery and other forms of oppression. Mitchell writes, "I am now convinced that the slaveocracy failed to erase African culture, but slowly succeed in getting Blacks to be ashamed of it. The result was that even though we Blacks continued to use and adapt our own heritage, we eventually dropped many aspects of it."[8]

Other experts concur with this assessment. John W. Blasingame agrees with Gayraud Wilmore's proposal that the more important inheritance of Black Americans from Africa is not musical or rhythmic but is in the nature of philosophy, worldview, and values in the word *religion*.[9] Blasingame, an authority on the enslaved community, provides this comment:

> The similarities between many European and African cultural elements enabled the slave to continue to engage in many traditional activities or to create a synthesis of European and African cultures. In the process of acculturation, the slaves made European forms serve African functions. An example of this is religion— Christian forms were so similar to African religious patterns that it was relatively easy for the early slaves to incorporate them with their traditional practices and beliefs. In America Jehovah replaced Creator, and Jesus replaced the Holy Ghost, and the Saints replaced all the lesser gods. After a few generations, the slaves forgot the African deities represented by the Judeo-Christian gods, but in many other facets of their religious services they retained many African elements.[10]

After Emancipation

Even as enslaved people, African Americans had attempted to provide financially, as well as spiritually, for family members. But, as Crable points out, after slavery ended, plantation-owners turned to "convict-leasing" to fill the gap in cheap labor. Black Codes, laws that severely restricted the rights of Black Americans, made it easy for the state to imprison them for petty offenses and then lease prisoners to plantation owners for a fee.

"After slavery, you see Black men and women taken away from their families, oftentimes for really minor, nonviolent crimes. It could be something as simple as not having a work pass," says Morgan.[11]

In addition, Blacks struggled to reunite families that had been disrupted by slavery. Family and kinship ties, together with the church, remained the foundation of the Black community.

The African American family has historically been intricately linked to the Black church. Phenomenologically the Black church in America developed out of the deprivation and oppression experienced by the enslaved men and women from Africa. The Black church existed as a support system. Mothers, fathers, sons, and daughters had been consistently sold away at masters' whims. The church evolved as a new family for those who were continually being uprooted from their original families.[12]

"He Ain't Heavy . . ."

The extended family has been the basis of the Black church from its inception. It is common for the laity of a congregation or even a denomination to address each other as brother or sister. This has been the protocol for pastors in addressing laity. The idea of the church as extended family has played a major role in the faith formation of African American adolescents. This has meant that family goes beyond bloodlines and includes all the members of the congregation. Members have taken on the responsibility of literally providing guidance and discipline as needed to children and youth of the congregation. This was more pronounced prior to the integration of schools.

However, national data do not support the popular myth that extended families have declined among African American families. On the contrary, the role of Black kinship networks has increased. Between 1970 and 1992, Black households with three generations rose from one out of four to one out of three. The Black extended family has informally adopted 800,000 children, while the government has not been able to find permanent homes for 200,000 Black children in foster care. Rates of child abuse are lowest among children reared by kin. In recognition of the increased importance of kin networks, child-welfare

A STORY FROM A YOUNG PERSON, GAIL:[14] I was pregnant and still in high school. I had been taken to church by my parents my entire life. One night my boyfriend and I lost total control and a few weeks later I discovered I was pregnant. My boyfriend, who told me he loved me and who I thought I loved, abandoned me when he found out I was pregnant. He went to college and I have not heard from him over these many years. I will never forget when I told my parents that I was pregnant. I could see that they were disappointed, but they talked to me calmly and assured me that they loved me. Of course, they asked questions about how I knew I was pregnant and wanted to know what I wanted to do.

My church had a large worshiping community, and it was easy sometimes to intentionally get lost in the crowd. I was so ashamed and embarrassed as it became more and more noticeable that I was pregnant. I no longer wanted to sing in the choir, for it felt like everyone was watching me. I felt I had let everyone down that cared about me. There were these two older female members of the church who were friends with my mother who came to me and encouraged me to continue to be faithful to God. They still are my number one supporters, and they are so kind to my child.

agencies have created a new category, "kinship care," to place children with relatives as their foster parents.

The Black church continues to have a positive impact on Black families. Research has found that Black youth who have positive outcomes as adults are those with strong religious commitments.[13] Family roles, kinship bonds, and religious orientation continue to be strengths of the Black family. A major part of that strength derives from the Black church that views itself as family. On many occasions I have heard people refer to the local congregation as their church family. No wonder when a person falls on hard times or death occurs in the family, the entire congregation rallies around that person. When a church member dies, the church family provides all kinds of care to the grieving family. It is not unusual for food items to be brought to the bereaving family's house each day up until the funeral.

Gail's story reminds me of a statement I once heard about youth ministry in regard to adults and their relationship to adolescents. The phrase "giving long loving looks at adolescents" was used in the context of speaking about adult responsibility to adolescents.[15] I once asked a group of adults in a study group to ponder this statement and did not receive a response. Later in that session one man said that was a deep question that made him recall his days as a teacher where he might have done better with some students who were rather disruptive.

It is critical for adolescents to experience the kind of love that holds on to one in the midst of a crisis and is long-lasting. One of the aspects of the relationship Gail shared with me was that the two women were non-judgmental. She was clear that these women exhibited a love for her more after she was pregnant than at any time in her life. They became her extended family.

Extended family and church-based social networks are important resources for African Americans because they provide social support to their members in the form of instrumental, emotional, social, and psychological assistance and resources.[16] Among African Americans, social networks provide informal support to address personal issues such as physical and mental health problems[17] and daily life stressors.[18]

In Gail's case extended family provided the social support needed for her to deal with the stress of being a pregnant adolescent. Gail's extended family went beyond what some definitions give for extended family such as "a family that includes in one household near relatives (such as grandparents, aunts, or uncles) in addition to a nuclear family."[19] The point is that in African American culture extended family is unique, largely because the extension includes but is not limited to members of Black congregations.

One of the great examples in Black culture concerning extended family is the "Divine Nine," the five Black Greek fraternities and four Black Greek sororities. Members in these organizations see each other as sisters and brothers, referring to each other as soror or frat. This has nothing to do with blood kinship, and all to do with brotherhood and sisterhood. Many of the members of the Divine Nine fraternities and sororities become members during their undergraduate work. Many choose to join graduate chapters, continuing after college with the sisterhood and brotherhood. A fair number join sororities and fraternities as adults of forty or fifty. Men and women proudly wear "their colors" throughout life, and when they die, a special ceremony is performed that formally places them in "the chapter of the eternal." The Divine Nine are undergirded with godly principles. Sometimes the kinship through these fraternal orders is stronger than that among blood relatives.

To illustrate how extended family occurs in the Black church and community, I tell this story from my adolescence. The church of my upbringing, Barrs Chapel CME Church, was located in rural northwest Tennessee. When I was a youth, I saw how the church and family intersected. Our home was probably the farthest away from the church, but we had a television, whereas other families did not. On Sunday nights a few people from our church would get in their cars and drive to our house to watch the then-popular TV show *Bonanza*. As I reflect, I recall that those who came to our house were not blood relatives, but they were Barrs Chapel CME Church members. It was out of that relationship that became a part of the extended family. A second memory is Bible study. A group of ladies of the church, some who were blood relatives and others who were not, would go from home to home monthly to study the Bible together. I vividly remember overhearing the ladies discuss the Bible and later enjoying some type of refreshment. These ladies of the church were extended family.

Recently, I read an article entitled "The Joy of Being Black and Having Extended Family" that had conversations with various Black people. One of the question-and-answer interchanges is a good example of the importance of extended family in Black culture.

Is there a specific memory that comes to mind when you think of the significance of your networks?

Kamelia: Five years ago, my sister passed away after a short battle with cancer. Towards the end, the hospital waiting room was filled with people. When we returned home from the hospital at 9 AM, my mum's house was filled to the brim with family and friends. Pots on the fire cooking food so we weren't hungry; others cleaning the house. Everyone rallied together and planned every fine detail of the funeral so that we as a family wouldn't have to. They took the kids for days out, so they weren't surrounded by sadness. It's a feeling I'll never forget. Being thrust into a situation like that is never easy for anybody, but to have that kind of support from the people of your community makes it that little bit more bearable.

Marcia: There is one memory that sticks out in my mind. I had a best friend who passed away some years ago, and I still remain really close to her children. When I came home from the hospital after my daughter passed, my best friend's son sat on my bed while I slept just to make sure I was okay. I know he did the same for my granddaughter too, as he understood what it was like to lose a parent. When my own mother

unfortunately passed away, my community came together and did it all again. No questions asked![20]

Adapting to Change

Extended family is important in Black culture. The strength of the
Black family is its extended nature. Smith makes the point that the two
skills that have allowed for the survival of the Black family, throughout
the period of slavery and beyond, are its extended nature and its adaptability to change.[21]

Sharecropping as an Example of Adaptability
Sharecropping is a type of farming in which families rent small plots
of land from a landowner in return for a portion of their crop, to be
given to the landowner at the end of each year. Different types of sharecropping have been practiced worldwide for centuries, but in the rural
South, it was typically practiced by former slaves and their descendants. With the southern economy in disarray after the abolition of
slavery and the devastation of the Civil War, conflict arose during the
Reconstruction era between many white landowners attempting to
reestablish a labor force and freed Blacks seeking economic independence and autonomy.

I have mixed memories of my mother and father as sharecroppers.
On the one hand, it was the means by which they provided for their
seven children and my maternal grandmother. The landowner seemed
to be a nice man. However, my father primarily did all of the work on
the farm in exchange for a house that was smaller than some apart-
ments where I have resided. My parents were always owing the
landowner. My mother worked in the fields to earn some money for
the household.

Adapting to changing conditions was the normal way of life. When
the television was no longer viewable, we listened to the radio. When
my father, the only one able to drive, could not take us to the bus stop
about one-half mile away, we would walk to that stop. When my fa-

ther was not able to meet us in the afternoon as we returned to that bus stop, we would get off the bus near our aunt's house and walk the one mile to her house, where she would feed us.

COVID-19 and Adaptability

As we write, the Black family is in the midst of yet another crisis, along with the entire world. COVID-19 has killed approximately one of every one thousand Black Americans—about twice the rate of death for white Americans. Research shows that COVID-19 kills men at nearly twice the rate of women. This is notable because men play an important role as husbands, fathers, and parental caretakers. The death of fathers causes single mothers to assume the role of providing for the children and, in many cases, taking care of elderly relatives without male support. Even for those whose partner does not succumb to the disease, many Black women face years of caring for a family member who might suffer from long-term complications. Such disruption, and the increased burden on Black women, connects to a long history of separation and disruption within the Black American family.[22]

How has the church made up of Black families adapted and changed during the pandemic? The answer is evolving. However, during the summer of 2020, we saw churches doing something different as they adapted to the changes necessitated by the global pandemic. A sterling example illustrative of this adaptation can be found in the celebration of a Pastor's Anniversary, a huge event in the Black church tradition. There is a unique role pastors play within the church and the larger community. The Pastor's Anniversary is a time to show the pastor, as well as the pastor's family, some special appreciation and love. Of course, this celebration most often takes place at the church or some other appropriate venue. During 2020, this could not be done. But the celebration continued as churches adapted. During the pandemic, it was not unusual to see cars lined up in front of pastors' houses or church parking lots as people paraded in their cars, leaving monetary gifts for the pastor and family. These celebrations extended to birthday and other special celebrations as the Black church adapted to maintain important traditions.

In the Black church tradition, people often stand in the sanctuary for extended times to talk after the worship service. It is called fellowship time. At the church I pastor, during the pandemic, worship was carried out virtually. Not long after we started this new way of worship, one of the young adults who had been formed in the church as an adolescent wrote me a note suggesting we try a new form of fellowship. So, from that point on, the church spends about thirty minutes of unplanned time just talking on Zoom. It has become the new form of fellowship.

One family in the church has adjusted during this pandemic by adding a monthly meeting via Zoom with all of their siblings. One member of that family told me that she knew they could not have the normal family reunion. Therefore, in order to stay in touch, they would spend time virtually, and that has led to the planning of a family reunion sometime in the future.

A Shift in the Meaning of Extended Family

A pastor tells this story. In a Sunday school class, one of the assistant teachers gently placed her hand on a little girl's shoulder to turn her in the direction that the teacher had instructed the class. The little girl reported to her mother that she doesn't like Sunday school anymore because the teacher's assistant was mean. The mother immediately confronted the teacher's assistant directly, telling her no one could put their hands on her child except her. The teacher's assistant explained the nature of the touch but was met with resistance from the mother, who told the assistant that she or no one at church had a right to correct her daughter without permission. This illustrates that no longer does the Black church have the automatic permission to form children through direct guidance. So, how in this century are African American adolescents being formed in the faith? We will next examine how spiritual formation and discipleship take place.

Spiritual Formation and Discipleship

The idea of family and church in Black culture is seen in how spiritual formation and discipleship take place. In an article in *Christianity Today*, findings from the Barna Group confirm my experience. Black believers are more likely to position their growth in Christ in the context of community and fellowship, while white Christians take a more individualized approach, according to the study released from Barna Research.[23] Black Christians also preferred group-based discipleship to one-on-one (32 percent versus 22 percent), while white Christians favored being discipled on their own (39 percent versus 31 percent), according to Barna. They are four times more likely than white Christians to list study groups as "very important" to their spiritual development.[24]

Barna's findings give rise to possibilities for Black churches to incorporate family ministry into their programs of Christian Education and Faith Formation. Specifically, the discovery or creation and utilization of discipleship curriculum designed for Black families are encouraged to facilitate the formation of disciples. I would strongly suggest that congregations or leaders provide a clear definition of what is meant by family to make sure no family structure is not considered. For instance, in the Black church, the bias of some might not consider two women with children as family.

Additionally, the findings offer the notion that to increase the involvement of Black youth in the life of the church, youth leaders and designers of curricula could collaborate to create innovative opportunities for forming Black youth across denominational lines and other demarcations. The global pandemic of 2020 and beyond has presented new opportunities to expand the Black church's reach. It might be such a time as this that the Black church begins a strong effort to combine its resources to provide small group study and formation opportunities for Black youth. This would include creating formation opportunities for youth that have no boundaries, such as local church and denomination. These church school meeting times would not be limited to Sunday.

The Barna study in 2017 revealed that

> the term "spiritual progress" is open to interpretation, and when asked to define it, differences in perspectives began to emerge between Black and white Christian leaders. Black Christian leaders were more likely to describe the process of spiritual progress as "spiritual maturation" (31 percent), while white Christian leaders preferred the phrase "spiritual growth" (21 percent). The language of "maturation" implies more of an internal transformation and the development of wisdom through life experience, whereas the word "growth" tends to suggest an approach that entails reaching key milestones.
>
> When both groups define "discipleship," white believers are more likely to refer to it as a "process of learning to follow Jesus Christ as Savior and Lord, seeking to observe all that Jesus commanded, by the power of the Holy Spirit and to his glory." Black Christians instead commonly refer to it as "the process of transformation that changes us to be increasingly more like Christ through the Word, the Spirit, and circumstance." For Black Christians, spiritual progress tends to focus more on life experience rather than achieving goals, about maturing into a Christ-like character as they weather life's storms.[25]

These findings suggest that there is a need for curricula designed specifically for Black youth. After nearly two decades of working as the leader of Christian Education and Formation for my denomination, I have concluded this task of creating curricula for our Black youth calls for an approach that has been difficult for the Black church. It is the combination of human resources. We who lead our various communions/denominations/fellowships are challenged to create a think tank that includes youth as welcomed voices to the table. Barna's findings around Black Christians' focus on life experience are very enlightening.

In my book *The Formation of a People,* I argue that this life experience is testimony and it is a way of Christian education. The Black church has an opportunity to use testimony in an intergenerational way. Youth can be placed in small group configurations that allow them to hear the testimonies of those who have varying life experiences, reciprocally sharing their own testimonies in return.

Barna researchers pointed out that fellowship was a particularly strong component of mentorship for African Americans. "There are plenty of similarities in how both groups define the primary goals of discipleship, but Black Christian leaders are more likely to say, 'deepening one's faith through education and fellowship' is a goal of discipleship (85 percent compared to 71 percent)."[26]

As a pastor in the Black church, I have discovered that eating (fellowship) and learning (education) is a good combination. Specifically, on various occasions, I have incorporated meals with a learning opportunity. This has included breakfast and church school taught by the pastor. Also, it has included lunch after the sermon and a short prepared and purposeful learning time. In one venue I discovered that coffee after the sermon and an informal discussion about the sermon to be effective.

In her summary of the Barna research, Mary Andlin writes,

> The group mindset among African Americans also stems from church history and current racial tensions. Black churches and denominations formed when their members were excluded from white fellowship. Given that Martin Luther King Jr.'s observation that Sunday at 11 a.m. is the most segregated hour in America mostly still holds true, believers continue to view these congregations as "a necessary place of refuge and

resistance" in the aftermath of racially motivated violence and systemic injustice, *Christianity Today* columnist Christena Cleveland wrote.

About a third of Black Christians and more than a quarter of white Christians say getting through tough times motivates them to pursue spiritual growth. These realities add significance to fellowship found in churches and small groups. While white Christians are more likely to label their spiritual lives as "entirely private," African Americans see their spiritual lives as intertwined with the social and political situations they face. Almost half of Black Christians (46 percent) believe their spiritual lives impact society at large, compared with 27 percent of white Christians.

An opportunity to enhance the spiritual growth and formation of Black youth is intentionally seeking out youth to be deliberate listeners to sermons delivered by the pastor. Designated youth would be asked to listen for themes of justice and how the socio-economic-political issues of the day are heard in the sermon. Pastors would be charged to invite youth to a small group to discuss their sermon and what the youth heard. Youth would be encouraged to provide their interpretations to the Scripture.

"There's something powerful about being together. It reminds me of a Henri Nouwen quote about the ministry of presence that suggests we underestimate just what being together means," Cleveland, discussing a retreat held for Christian women of color last year. "Often, we want to preach eloquent sermons or produce some sort of amazing artistic expression to touch people's hearts, and that's great . . . but a lot of it is laughing and knowing that we're not alone."[27]

A wise pastor once told me that a good gauge to measure the health of the congregation is what happens after the benediction. He said that if people lingered around in the sanctuary for long periods of time after the benediction, that is a sign of a healthy congregation. During the pandemic, in the church I serve as pastor, when we returned to the building, in our efforts to social distance, we allowed people to enter one door and exit another door. People were reminded constantly not to linger in the sanctuary, but to exit immediately. That modality lasted a few weeks and almost automatically people started lingering in the sanctuary. People wanted to laugh together.

Black churches are encouraged to create spaces for youth to gather and laugh together. I experienced one Black youth minister creating electronic games that occurred at designated times. I observed much talking and laughing as youth engaged in these games. I have seen how youth have been able to conduct church business asynchronously.

Moreover, the Barna researchers observed,

> Black communities tend toward communal rhythms of spiritual development while white communities prefer a more individualistic setting. It is unsurprising therefore that white Christians are more likely to view their spiritual life as "entirely private" (42 percent compared to 32 percent). Black Christians, on the other hand, are much more likely to believe their personal spiritual life has an impact on others—whether they are relatives, friends, community, or society at large. For instance, Black Christians are much more likely to believe that their personal spiritual lives have an impact on broader society (46 percent compared to 27 percent).
>
> This was a strong belief of Martin Luther King, and it appears to have had great staying power. He fundamentally believed that one's personal spiritual life had implications for societal justice, and he called

Christians—on both sides of the debate—to bring
their faith to bear on the struggle for civil rights, to
which he dedicated his life. This impact is also tied to
the approach to evangelism: half of Black Christians
(50 percent compared to 34 percent) believe it is their
responsibility to tell others about their religious beliefs, further reinforcing the public/private contrast between both groups.[28]

As I was writing these words, I glanced at my Facebook page and
was left shaking my head. The headline read, "An active shooter at an
elementary school down the street." I began to wonder who prayed
this morning, read Scripture, or thought about God as the day began.
What spiritual tools do parents, teachers, administrators, and family
members have that will assist during this present reality?

A quick review of the focus or mission of a few historical Black denominations along with two diverse congregations affirms the public
emphasis of the Black church, small group ministry, and thus the extended family's importance in the Black church. Below are some snip-
pets from the websites of those churches.

The African Methodist Episcopal Church
In order to meet the needs of every level of the connection and in every
local church, the AME Church shall implement strategies to train all
members in: (1) Christian discipleship, (2) Christian leadership, (3)
current teaching methods and materials, (4) the history and significance
of the AME Church, (5) God's biblical principles, and (6) social development to which all should be applied to daily living.[29]

The African Methodist Episcopal Zion Church
The mission of the African Methodist Episcopal Zion Church is to increase our love for God and meet humankind by "loving God with all
the heart, with all our soul, with all our mind and to love our neighbor
as ourselves."[30]

Christian Methodist Episcopal Church
The mission of the Christian Methodist Episcopal Church is to be disciples of Jesus the Christ by serving individuals, communities, and the world as the representative, loving presence of God and as witnesses to God's salvation and grace.[31]

National Baptist Convention
The mission of the Convention is to fulfill the Great Commission of Jesus Christ through preaching, teaching, and healing.[32]

American Baptist Churches USA
American Baptists are Christ-centered, biblically grounded, ethnically diverse people called to radical personal discipleship in Christ Jesus. "Our commitment to Jesus propels us to nurture authentic relationships with one another; build healthy churches; transform our communities, our nations, and our world; engage every member in hands-on ministry; and speak the prophetic word in love."[33]

United Church of Christ
"To love God with all our heart, mind, soul, and strength and our neighbor as ourselves."[34]

Conclusion

From its inception in America, the Black church has been strongly intertwined with the Black family. This relationship has been the result of the idea of extended family that does not limit family to blood relatives. Black adolescents come from a variety of blood-relative family structures but are not limited to those structures. The extended family remains important in the life of the Black church. Adaptation to change has historically been a strength of the Black church and family. The need for adaptability has been exacerbated by the global pandemic, yet the Black church and family have shown resiliency.

A strength of the Black family that translates into the Black church is a strong "kinship bond." It is part of the concept of extended family. I recall a time when the parents of my grandchildren needed someone to see that their son could attend a special event because of their conflicting schedules. They sent out an inquiring group text to the family, including grandparents, church members, and siblings. Of course they got some positive responses. Family unity and kinship bonds create a sense of belonging to a network of supportive individuals or groups that respect and nurture strengths.

The importance of the family in the life of the Black church is to be celebrated. A commitment to the Black family generates strength, stability, and love in the Black church. Conversely, the strength of the Black family is the Black church. A strong religious orientation has historically provided support to the Black family, especially in times of crisis. Having experienced the death of close family members, I have often said to congregations that I really don't know how people can deal with death without a relationship in some way with God.

Another strength of the Black family that gives strength to the Black church is a desire to achieve in spite of obstacles. This is part of the persevering spirit that leads to the ability to bounce back against the greatest of odds.

Question: List as many family configurations as you can (e.g., dual family, single family). What role does the family play in the faith formation of Black adolescents?

NOTES

1. Harriet McAdoo, "Interpreting the Afro-American Heritage in the Afro-American Family Organization," in *Black Families*, ed. Niara Suderkass (Thousand Oaks, CA: Sage, 1981), 40.

2, Wallace C. Smith, *The Church in the Life of the Black Family* (Valley Forge, PA: Judson Press, 1990), 30.

3. Thomas Lewis, "Transatlantic Slave Trade," updated August 18, 2021, Britannica, https://www.britannica.com/topic/transatlantic-slave-trade.

4. "The Enslaved Family," in The Making of African American Identity: volume 1, 1500–1865, National Humanities Center, Toolbox Library: Primary Resources in U.S. History and Literature, 2007, http://nationalhumanitiescenter.org/pds/maai/community/text1/text1read.htm.

5. Jennifer Hallam, "The Slave Experience: Family," Thirteen, 2004, https://www.thirteen.org/wnet/slavery/experience/family/history.html.

6. Margaret Crable, "The Pandemic Echoes a History of Disruption for Black Families, Stretching Back to Slavery," March 19, 2021, USC Dornsife, https://dornsife.usc.edu/news/stories/3429/the-pandemic-echoes-a-history-of-disruption-for-Black-families-s/.

7. Henry H. Mitchell, *Black Belief: Folk Beliefs of Blacks in America and West Africa* (New York: Harper and Row, 1975), 9.

8. Ibid., 20.

9. John W. Blasingame, *The Slave Community: Plantation Life in the Antebellum South* (New York: Oxford University Press, 1972), 17–18.

10. Ibid., 10.

11. Crable; the quotation in Crable's article is from Alisa Morgan, assistant professor of history at the USC Dornsife College of Letters, Arts and Sciences.

12. Smith, 22.

13. Robert B. Hill, "A 'Strengths Perspective' on Black Families," July 21, 1997, *The Baltimore Sun*, https://www.baltimoresun.com/news/bs-xpm-1997-07-21-1997202116-story.html.

14. Her name has been changed to protect her privacy.

15. This phrase is an adaptation of the phrase from Ignatian spirituality: "giving a long loving look at the real" (Vinita Hampton Wright).

16. N. Krause and E. Bastida, "Church-based Social Relationships, Belonging, and Health among Older Mexican Americans," *Journal for the Scientific Study of Religion* 50, no. 2 (January 2011): 397–409; R. J. Taylor, L. M. Chatters, and J. Levin, *Religion in the Lives of African Americans: Social, Psychological, and Health Perspectives* (Thousand Oaks, CA: Sage, 2004).

17. S. Cohen, L. Brittney, and B. H. Gottlieb, *Social Support Measurement and Intervention: A Guide for Health and Social Scientists* (New York: Oxford University Press, 2000); R. J. Taylor, D. H. Chae, K. D. Lincoln, and L. M. Chatters, "Extended Family and Friendship Support Networks Are Both Protective and Risk Factors for Major Depressive Disorder, and Depressive Symptoms among African Americans and Black Caribbeans," *Journal of Nervous and Mental Disease* 203 (2015): 132–40.

18. M. Benin and V. M. Keith, "The Social Support of Employed African American and Anglo Mothers," *Journal of Family Issues* 16 (1995): 275–97.

19. "Extended family," Merriam-Webster, https://www.merriam-webster.com/dictionary/extended%20family.

20. Elete Nelson-Fearon, "The Joy of Being Black and Having Extended Family," November 29, 2020, Vice, https://www.vice.com/en/article/xgz893/the-joy-of-being-Black-and-having-an-extended-family.

21. Smith, 22.

22. See Crable; Dani McClain, "How Black Parents Survived 2020," December 22, 2020, https://www.nytimes.com/2020/12/22/parenting/Black-parents-pandemic.html.

23. Kate Shellnut, "How Black and White Christians Do Discipleship Differently," January 13, 2017, *Christianity Today*, https://www.christianitytoday.com //news/2017/january/how-Black-white-christians-discipleship-differently.html.

24. Ibid.

25. "Racial Divides in Spiritual Practices," January 12, 2017, Barna, https://www.barna.com/research/racial-divides-spiritual-practice/.

26. Ibid.

27. Mary Andlin, "How Black and White Christians Do Discipleship Differently," January 17, 2017, Gospel Minds, https://gospelminds.com/blog/Black-white-christians-discipleship-differently/. For the quote about segregation in worship, see Martin Luther King Jr., "The Most Segregated Hour in America," https://www.youtube.com/watch?v=1q881g1L_d8. This clip is from an interview in which King discusses how church segregation is inconsistent with Jesus' life and message of reconciliation.

28. "Racial Divides in Spiritual Practices."

29. "Church Mission," The African Methodist Episcopal Church, https://www.ame-church.com/our-church/our-mission/.

30. "Church Mission," The African Methodist Episcopal Church, https://www.ame-church.com/our-church/our-mission/.

31. "Our Mission Statement," The Christian Methodist Episcopal Church, https://thecmechurch.org/mission-beliefs/.

32. "Mission and Objectives," The National Baptist Convention, USA, Inc., https://www.nationalbaptist.com/about-nbc/mission-objectives.

33. "ABCUSA Mission Statement," American Baptist Churches USA, http://www.abc-usa.org/mission-statement.

34. "Purpose Statement (from the Gospel of Matthew)," United Church of Christ, https://www.ucc.org/mission/.

Chapter 7

Now What?

Looking Ahead

It is through the lens of a change in the ethos that we listened to the stories of adolescents today two to three generations removed from legal segregation who, nevertheless, often find segregation to be a reality even when it appears not to exist. We further wanted to listen to these stories to see how African American adolescents' identities are being formed, specifically related to the formation of faith.

We led focus groups involving several dozen young adults who grew up in the Black church, asking about their adolescent experience in the church. We hoped that being a few years removed from the experience might offer perspective and reflection. We listened further to their stories to hear how the relationships of the twenty-first century might be distinct from earlier centuries in the Black church. It is our belief that in listening to these stories, we might find a key to understanding faith formation in African American adolescents.

For perspective, in addition to listening to the voices of younger folks, we listened to the voices of the past as we began this book surveying the rich history of the Black church. When I visited the National Museum of African American History and Culture, I experienced a connection to my ancestors. It is my belief that we do ourselves a worthy service to survey our Black church history. Conversations with members of focus groups affirmed that part of the uniqueness of the Black church is found in the bonds of its community and its rich history. The search for the faith formation of Black adolescents begins with our history. Before we can look forward, we must look backward. This is Sankofa, which expresses the importance of reaching back to knowledge gained in the past and bringing it into the present in order to make positive progress.

As we move forward in the twenty-first century, education of Black adolescents will remain a crucial aspect of their faith formation journey. In the public sector Black youth overall are lagging behind their white counterparts when it comes to education. A report in *U.S. News* says that educational expectations are lower for Black children, according to Child Trends, a non-profit and non-partisan research center that tracks data about children. Black parents, most of whom are less educated than their white counterparts, don't expect their children to attain as much education as white parents expect. Lower expectations become self-fulfilling prophecies, contributing to lower expectations from the student, less-positive attitudes toward school, fewer out-of-school learning opportunities, and less parent-child communication about school.[1] As the Black church moves forward, it is challenged to pay attention and effect changes to public education in the United States. If our youth struggle with reading, they will also struggle in our efforts to nurture them in the church, providing faith formation.

Ultimately, the Black church's pro-activist approach with public education contributes to the actions and experiences that eventually lead to the faith formation of Black adolescents. Part of the process of transforming the lives of adolescents begins with education. One of the ways the Black church can assist public education is the involvement in the Children's Defense Fund (CDF) child advocacy efforts, including Freedom Schools. Over the last several years, I have become involved with the Children's Defense Fund, whose mission is "to ensure every child a healthy start, a head start, a fair start, a safe start and a moral start in life and successful passage to adulthood with the help of caring families and communities." CDF Freedom Schools empower youth to "excel and believe in their ability to make a difference in themselves, their families, communities, country and world with hope, education and action."[2]

Rooted in the Mississippi Freedom Summer project of 1964, the CDF Freedom Schools program is a six-week summer literacy and cultural enrichment program designed to serve children and youth in grades K–12 in communities where quality academic enrichment programming is limited, too expensive, or non-existent. By partnering with schools, faith and community-based organizations, municipalities, colleges and universities, and juvenile detention facilities, the Freedom School program is offered in these communities at no cost.

The CDF Freedom Schools program enhances children's motivation to read and makes them feel good about learning. At the same time, the program connects families to the right resources in their communities. Freedom School students engage in a research-based, multicultural Integrated Reading Curriculum that supports them and their families through five essential components:

1. High-quality academic enrichment
2. Parent and family development
3. Civic engagement and social action
4. Intergenerational servant leadership development
5. Nutrition, health, and mental health

Students also receive two nutritious meals and a snack daily, as well as a book each week to build their home libraries.

The program believes in an intergenerational leadership model. That's why the program is staffed primarily by college students and recent college graduates, with a 10:1 child to adult ratio. As a result, many children and youth make significant gains in reading achievement and don't experience any summer learning loss.[3]

During the summer of 2019, the church I pastor sponsored and executed a CDF Freedom School. In the first six weeks (thirty program days), we engaged twenty-nine second-graders, and we documented improvement in their literacy. The church's experience affirmed the understanding of extended family. The church was able to involve students from a local historically Black college and university, high school students, middle, and elementary students. It was a great example of intergenerational ministry. As the Black church marches forward in the twenty-first century, it is challenged to build on its extended family and church heritage.

During our focus group research, a young adult, Tim, spoke about the influence of older persons in his life, and how he was attracted to their strong foundation. Several adolescents experienced this during our 2019 CDF Freedom School, developing positive relationships with someone older. The benefits of such relationships across generations help each see the humanity and the gifts of the other.

Along this line of thinking, as we look forward, the Black church can continue to expand its understanding of the church and family by implementing programs that provide opportunities for Black adolescents to experience extended family. In the early 1990s I created such a program that continues to be used. "Enlightened Males" (EM) grew out of my deep care and concern for African American adolescent males at this critical juncture in their lives. Having journeyed that way myself some years ago, I felt compassion for this poignant moment in the developmental process of our Black sons. My research in this area brought me to the conviction that, beginning in adolescence, identity is formed through increasingly taking agency for one's own choices. For African American boys, gender and culture are two key aspects of identity formation during adolescence.

Enlightened Males (for young men ages ten to seventeen) is a year-long program that involves meeting with a group of boys twice a month for three hours, going on field trips together, meeting and talking with their parents (mothers mainly), and visiting some of their churches. The program culminates with a rite-of-passage program. This program's success depends on the volunteerism of church members and other interested people. Convinced of the importance of positive African American adult male role models to aid in their journeys, the EM program was designed to surround the boys with such men—from pillar organizations in the African American context like congregations, the community, and African American fraternities. Since formation involves continual shaping and traditioning in a way of being and doing, rites of passage and ritual were woven into the EM program from its inception. Peer mentoring and leadership was another important aspect of the program, and boys who completed the rite of passage were invited to join the group of adult men in leading the program the next year (with the added benefit of continuing those beneficial mentoring relationships).

We asked young adults in our focus groups: "Who are the people in your life that are largely responsible for how you feel about God? What makes them special to you?" One response stands out from a participant I will call Rachel. She talked about how she came to the church as a teenager through the invitation of a friend:

> I had trouble relating to the church at first, because I didn't know much about it. But the pastor was so kind and friendly. She invited me to lunch one day, and we had such a beautiful conversation. I was hesitant at first to accept her invitation because I knew I was still in "the world." I only came to church because my friend told me it would be fun. Although I was having fun there, I still felt guilty in a way because I just didn't think I was good enough to be in a church. I guess the pastor sensed something because she was friendly the first time I met her. After going to lunch she checked on me each week to see if I was okay. I have been at church now for two years, and she still checks on me. I guess you could say she is mentoring me.

Rachel went on to say, "Pastor met me where I was; made me feel safe. I could talk to her and I felt safe. She was non-judgmental." Relationships keep people coming back. For Rachel, her relationship with the pastor kept her coming to the church.

When my children were teens, the young adults of the church I served as pastor decided to make it their ministry to mentor the youth of the church. The young adult female who took on the assignment of mentoring my daughter did such a good job of nurturing that, though my daughter is now past the young adult age, her former mentor has grown into one of her closest friends. Giving time is the most important task of parents and church members.

A young man that I will call Larry expressed how seeing his mother handle the household had a great impact on his direction in life. "She raised me to be a functional adult." He went on talk about the importance of relationships and shared about the high level of respect he had for some people in the church that he called surrogate grandparents. He especially spoke of teachers as mentors.

Social Justice

Our research tells us that adolescents are concerned with issues of social justice. They want to make a difference in the world. I started seeing this taking place in the early 2000s within my denomination working with young adults. Each time they gathered in church meetings they planned ways to provide some service to the local community.

Social justice is defined by Black adolescents today in a somewhat different way it was in the 1950s and 1960s. When asked, "What does it mean to hear the phrase 'the struggle' as it relates to Black people?" answers from our focus group participants weren't the ones we might have heard from those of the civil rights era that dealt with issues of racism and discrimination. They were a desire to protest against the violence perpetrated against Blacks by police. Television media, social media, and the advent of phones with cameras have led to greater awareness of police brutality and assaults on the lives of Black people. Protests have mounted to bring attention and justice to these atrocities.

Although the responses did not negate those as real and something we should forget, they did talk about "the struggle" in a different way. Their voices gave the impression that today as young people they face different issues from those faced by people in the 1950s and 1960s. One group focused on younger people growing older faster. For example, one person observed that a mother she knows gives her nine-year-old daughter a credit card to use when she goes to visit her grandmother out of town. One focus group spent quite a bit of time talking about the ways they struggle today, particularly with police violence toward African Americans. As the person speaking was describing ways his generation struggled today that elders didn't, another participant reminded him of the water cannons and dogs used by police on elders during the civil rights struggle. "Maybe our struggle isn't so different," he reflected. Another focus group participant spoke about young children who go home after school and there is no adult present. Some spoke of parents working long hours as a way of the struggle materially. Some even mentioned financial and family security as a struggle. In these cases, the struggle is not new—perhaps this tells us something about the universality of the experience of being Black in the United States and a connection shared across generations that might lead to greater cohesion.

The Black adolescents in our research are concerned about civil rights, but that is not what dominates their thinking when it comes to justice. Inclusion is a major issue. However, it seems to me, based on what we heard in our research, intersectionality is a phenomenon that the Black church will encounter through Black adolescents. Intersectionality is the theory that the overlap of various social identities, such as race, gender, sexuality, and class, contributes to the specific type of systemic oppression and discrimination experienced by an individual. It is the oppression and discrimination resulting from the overlap of an individual's various social identities.[4]

> The increasing application of intersectionality to the psychological study of identity development raises questions regarding how researchers construct and use social identity categories, as well as how we best capture and address systems of oppression and priv-

ilege within our work. The continental European context helps us consider how we understand race differently in the American context. In Europe the use of the intersectionality paradigm "race" was officially removed from the vernacular following the atrocities of WWII, yet racialized oppression continues to occur in Europe at every level of society. Even without the language of race, the oppression of systemic racism occurs. Participants in our study seemed to be reflecting this understanding in many of their responses.[5]

One way the Black church can assist and involve adolescents in social justice is by ensuring each one is engaged with the NAACP youth programs. The goal of the NAACP is to ensure a society in which all individuals have equal rights without discrimination based on race by developing a new generation of civil rights and community leaders.

The aim of the NAACP is to

■ Inform youth of the problems affecting African Americans and other racial and ethnic minorities

■ Advance the economic, educational, social, and political status of African Americans and other racial and ethnic minorities, and their harmonious cooperation with other people

■ Stimulate an appreciation of the African Diaspora and other people of color's contribution to civilization

■ Develop an intelligent, effective youth leadership[6]

Parental Involvement Extended

To state the importance of parents in the lives of youth is obvious. Yet, it has too often been my experience it must be emphasized. Earlier in this chapter I mentioned the CDF Freedom Schools and the Enlightened Males programs. These programs are designed to have regular meetings with the parents of the participant in the programs.

It is important, as well, for parents to be involved in the spiritual lives and choices of their adolescent children. The National Study on Youth and Religion (NSYR) and two of the books it spawned, *Soul Searching* by Christian Smith and Melinda Lundquist Denton, and *Almost Christian* by Kenda Dean, affirm that teenagers for the most part live out a faith that looks very much like the faith of their parents. Thus, parents who actively disciple their children raise children who in most cases have an active faith life. Parents, according to this massive research study, are the primary educators of youth. No surprise there for many who are involved with the faith formation of adolescents.

Two participants in one of our focus groups are preacher's kids (PKs) who are very active in the church. They spoke about the influence of their mom and dad, talking about how they taught them through precept and example. The conversation reminded me of my dad and mom, whom I never remember sitting me down and giving me lectures but living a life that represented what they prayed and taught about at church.

Others in focus groups talked about their parents as well. It was most moving to hear about the dads because so often dads in Black families are stereotyped in negative ways. One commented, "My dad impacted my experience." Further elaboration helped show this meant the dad was one who openly shared his experiences in life as testimonies.

Many in the focus groups described their experience of having parents who were absent from their spiritual lives. In those cases, the church filled the void, thus giving affirmation to extended families. Some spoke of the influence of their pastor, and others spoke in raving tones about their grandmothers and church mothers who had great faith. Even others spoke of a Sunday school teacher who was a mentor. Even though they did not use the words, they were affirming the extended family.

Faith Formation

As the Black church moves forward, it must take a serious look at faith formation. It must listen to the voices of adolescents and value their insights. Some participants in our focus groups offered insights like these:

- "I did less and I didn't participate much in the church (I was bad)."
- "I was not a part of the youth group. I was given the choice and chose not to be involved."
- "I was involved only for selfish reasons to get service points."
- "There was much talk about what I do. Not any talk about what was being formed."

This last statement caused me to reflect on the assumption we often make when we ask adolescents a question like, "What do you want to be when you grow up?" by which we mean, "What do you want to do?" I was reminded of a devotional I read many years ago from Chuck Swindoll in which he offers the following: "Without wanting to sound needlessly critical, as I look back over three decades, I think we were asked to answer the wrong question. What we want to *do* is not nearly as important as what we want to *be*."

I have seen "doing" devoid of reflection become overemphasized too often in youth ministry. I have listened to many reports from youth ministers and adult ministers that tout the doing, such as trips taken or service offered. However, rarely have I heard in these brag sessions reports made of how faith formation has taken place in the life of youth. Faith formation activities such as Sunday school classes cannot become just another item on the to-do list if faith formation is truly our goal. Intentionality is key in effective and transformative faith formation.

"Teaching for transformation considers that some information is important but that information or knowledge for its own sake isn't enough. When we teach for transformation, we go beyond sharing information to inviting participants to consider and discern together how the information impacts our lives and choices."[7]

The problem isn't the doing itself. It's that the service or trips take place without a clear and concrete connection made to one's faith. And it's not enough to pray before meals and sing some Jesus-y songs. Drawing the connections clearly means making explicit that we serve others in all places and times in our lives, not just mission trips, and that we do so because of the mandate of our faith to care for neighbors and to welcome especially those (in Bible times, it was widows, orphans, resident aliens) without rights and without recourse in our culture. And serving doesn't stop with giving out food—it extends to asking why there are poor or homeless people and then acting to bring equity and justice. Doing can definitely be transformative, but it takes intentionality. Transformative faith formation is not a program—it's a way of life!

Addressing Gun Violence

As I write, flashing across the news wire is information about another mass shooting in the United States. Black adolescents not only hear this news but also find themselves or those they know as victims. As we move forward in the Black church, we must ask ourselves what our role should be. The mass shootings are news headlines, but it is well documented that gun violence in this country is disproportionately visited upon the bodies and the souls of dark-skinned people. So our work is to recover and understand that historical legacy of violence. Every day, the number of individuals killed in this country by guns equals a mass shooting. We have a school bus worth of gun violence victims every day—thirty-three, thirty-four a day. They are disproportionately Black males. We have a country with a gun violence epidemic.[8] When you look at race and violence across the world, two things seem to be different about our country: the availability of guns without any meaningful regulations and the legacies of slavery and structural racism.

Michael McBride, the national director of the Lifelines to Healing/LIVE FREE Campaign, a faith-based effort to address gun violence and mass incarceration of young people of color, says, "The church has a critical role to play in the effort to address gun violence—helping to create peaceful communities. . . . And the church must lead the way in transforming such neighborhoods into places of true peace, justice and inclusion."[9]

Gun violence is an assault on our humanity and faith. The Black church is challenged to advocate for gun control and to lobby politically for the same. What the Black church has directly in its control is the prophetic message, the gospel of peace. Black adolescents should hear preachers in the fashion of the Old Testament prophets responding to the evils of their day with a dedicated and constant voice. Like the prophets, preachers today should refuse to let their calls for justice be silenced. Their voices represent God's voice as they communicate God's word to the people. True prophets don't speak on their own authority, but rather deliver the message they hear from God. They dare to speak truth to power, whether secular or religious.

Worship, Music, and Adolescents

Our research was clear. Music is extremely important in the lives of Black adolescents. Many adolescents live their lives with headphones or earbuds constantly playing music like a soundtrack for their lives. Many can't fall asleep without music playing. When asked about worship, one focus group member responded, "Friends say, 'I don't like church, but I like the music.' I think it is because it is gospel or soul. It is different from other expressions. Music makes you move."

However, the actions and love for music did not start with this new generation. In the 1970s, youth had boom boxes that they carried around with them; they played loud music in dormitory rooms and cars; and they participated in parties with loud music, then sang in the church choir on Sundays. Before that, songs were sung *a capella*, and before that, spirituals sung in hush arbors.

African American music cannot be separated from the rich cultures of Africa or from the forced transportation of millions of African people across the Atlantic who were then enslaved. The cultures from which they were torn and the conditions into which they were forced both contributed to the sounds of African American music. Many of the instruments historically used in African American music, including the banjo and the drum, have antecedents in African musical instruments, and many features common to African American music likewise have roots in African musical traditions, such as the call-and-response song form and an immersive approach to singing.[10] "Please understand that all African American religious music is not spiritual or gospel," according to Dr. James ("Jimmie") Abbington.

Although spirituals and gospel music have contributed songs now used in almost every denomination in North America, the body of African American church music is much broader. More than thirty Black pastors and church musicians, including Abbington, worked for eight years to compile 575 songs from the major Black Protestant hymnals into one volume, the African American Heritage Hymnal. This hymnal represents all the genres of African American church music.[11]

The point here is that music is important and central to African American culture and religion. Connecting to all generations' realities continues to be challenging. However, all generations must be included if the worship experience is to reflect the values of our faith. The challenge to the Black church is to be welcoming to all forms of music.

We asked in the focus groups, "What moves you in worship?" A member of the focus group I call Lydia said, "It speaks to me." Other expressions from the focus group included

- "I learn but I am not moved." We followed up, "What do you feel when people shout?"
- "They are getting in touch with God."
- "My personality won't allow me to shout."
- "Service is subject to change due to the Holy Spirit."
- "I was in a service where this happened, and people shouted for an hour."
- "I said it was unacceptable from the old Methodist context."

- "Sincerity means much for it."
- "Outward expression and then what is the next thing."

According to Anne Wimberly,

> Black Christian worship is a dynamic communal or "village" participatory event centered on hope. As a communal event, Black worship is an experience of people's conversational connection with God's hope for them, responding to this hope, and envisioning ways of acting on it beyond worship. From quiet contemplation to zestful body movement or rhythmic motion, singing, shouting, testifying, praying, and responding during the preached word, the community praises God, lays before God their personal and corporate stories of plight and possibility, and attests to and offers to act on God's plans for their future with hope.[12]

Wimberly's definition leads to the thought that there is room for everyone in worship. It seems to me this is the time that the Black church should be looking for collaborative efforts in planning and leading worship. More intentionality is needed to develop worship teams that will rise to the vibrancy of worship.

Conclusion

I was part of a listening tour for my denomination. One night, a group of Black youth gathered to respond to the denomination's strategic planning document. Reverberating out of the dialogue were the reactions of the youth, which can be summed up with three words: respect, accountability, and representation.

When asked to make comments about the denomination's plan that was presented, it seemed that it was too wordy for them. Some said when it is presented in that manner, they find it boring. They even said it needed to be delivered to them from younger people who knew what youth liked.

As I listened to the youth respond and react, I kept thinking to myself that we have come a mighty long way as the Black church. It was an unprecedented moment for the denomination to solicit the feedback from youth. We adults thought specifically asking for youth feedback was enough for a first step, but these youth were under-impressed. They wanted a chance to sit at the table where the decisions were being made. This is what they meant by representation. Although I am not convinced youth sitting at this particular table will be effective, as there are already more than thirty people on the task force, I am not opposed to that request. I wonder if what they really want might be to create their own table . . . I believe the first step is to help youth feel a sense of ownership. That requires time, sometimes a hard commodity to find.

When asked what they meant by accountability, they said it means to do what we ask for you to do. That's a fairly one-sided response but not atypical of the adolescent developmental stage that can still be somewhat self-focused at times. I wonder about the role of mutual accountability reflected in the values of our faith.

The last expectation is respect. They want to be heard and involved. They said their ideas were not taken seriously. This is a challenge for adults, and especially for baby boomers who hold many positions of power in the church right now. Baby boomers in the Black context were raised to understand young people's role was to be seen and not heard. This does not work for youth of more recent generations. They have grown up with technology and social media to make their voices heard and, as mentioned earlier, they are deeply concerned about social justice. They will not be silenced. They have too many means to communicate for them not to be heard. They speak through many digital platforms, including text messaging and social media. They access people 24/7/365.

As the Black church moves forward in its ministry with Black adolescents, one of the biggest challenges it faces is making the church one that radically accepts Black youth for who they are. This means doing ministry with youth and not always to youth. During the global pandemic of 2020 and forward, the Black church has had the opportunity to use the gifts of Black youth at a different level. At the forefront of that opportunity is the area of technology. In just a few days, technologically native youth became crucial to the ability of the church to continue to worship safely distanced via virtual platforms. Over the course of the last year, they have served and equipped congregations engaging the virtual space for the first time. I hope we have learned that Black adolescents may need the Black church, but the Black church needs Black adolescents, as well. The church must be willing to open its doors in ways that may be unfamiliar, but necessary to reach those who are seeking. And what higher calling could the church have?

Question: How can social justice movements, such as Black Lives Matter, foster strong church relations?

NOTES

1. "Who We Are," Child Trends, https://www.childtrends.org/about-us; Lindsey Cook, "U.S. Education: Still Separate and Unequal," January 28, 2015, *U.S. News*, https://www.usnews.com/news/blogs/data-mine/2015/01/28/us-education-still-separate-and-unequal.

2. "CDF Freedom Schools® Program Overview," Children's Defense Fund, https://www.childrensdefense.org/programs/cdf-freedom-schools/.

3. "The CDF Freedom Schools Model," Children's Defense Fund, https://www.childrensdefense.org/programs/cdf-freedom-schools/about-the-program/.

4. "Intersectionality," Dictionary.com, https://www.dictionary.com/browse/intersectionality.

5. Ursula Moffitt, Linda P. Juang, and Moin Syed, "Intersectionality and Youth Identity Development in Europe," *Psychology* 31 (January 2020), Frontiers in Psychology, https://www.frontiersin.org/articles/10.3389/fpsyg.2020.00078/full.

6. "Our Voice, Our Vision," NAACP, https://naacp.org/our-work/youth-programs/youth-college.

7. Denise Janssen, *Fostering Faith: Teaching and Learning in the Christian Church* (Valley Forge, PA: Judson Press 2014), 36.

8. Michael McBride, "Gun Violence, Race, and the Church," February 7, 2017, Faith and Leadership, https://faithandleadership.com/michael-mcbride-gun-violence-race-and-church.

9. Ibid.

10. "Roots of African American Music," *Smithsonian*, https://www.si.edu/spotlight/african-american-music/roots-of-african-american-music.

11. Joan Huyser-Honig and James Abbington, "African American Church Music: Beyond the Myths," May 14, 2014, Calvin Institute of Christian Worship, https://worship.calvin.edu/resources/resource-library/african-american-church-music-beyond-the-myths.

12. Anne E. Streaty Wimberly, "Worship in the Lives of Black Adolescents: Builder of Resilience and Hope," *Liturgy* 29, no. 1 (2014): 23–33, https://www.tandfonline.com/doi/abs/10.1080/0458063X.2014.846742.

Chapter 8

Can These Bones Live?

Pentecost Sunday 2021, I preached from Ezekiel 37:1-14 to ask the question from that text, "Can these bones live?" I began the sermon by reminding the congregation of the number of mass shootings over the last few years and the lives lost or injured as a result. On Pentecost weekend, CNN reported there were at least twelve mass shootings across the United States; Headline News reported eight more people shot dead the following Tuesday in a San Jose railyard. I raised concern about the vast amount of the wealth in the world that is held in the hands of fewer than one hundred individuals. I went on to make a case for the number of Black lives lost to shootings by police. I noted the number of homicides that happen every day in small and large cities. I went on to say that we live in a culture where we, like the people in Babylonian exile in the sixth century B.C.E., are dry bones, once marrow-filled skeletons, created by God, now picked clean by a culture intent on death for many rather than life for all. We live in a death-dealing culture.

What I did not mention in the sermon but is most worthy of mention during the twenty-first century is that on March 25, 2021, Georgia state senator, Park Cannon, a Black woman, was arrested for knocking on the door of the private office of Brian Kemp, the governor of Georgia, as he and six white men signed a law that effectively suppressed the right of Black people to vote in local, state, and federal elections.

Cannon was charged with two felony counts of obstruction of law enforcement and disruption of the General Assembly. Again, I say, we live in a death-dealing culture.

Why raise these concerns and issues while writing a book about faith formation of Black adolescents? My answer is simple. From my vantage point these things epitomize a death culture. In the midst of all this death, the Black church is called to offer life. This call comes from Black adolescents who struggle to find meaning in the church and are looking at social justice in an intersectional way while at the same time dealing with the effects of white supremacy and racism. Black youth want to know what faith in God has to do with all of the many issues and concerns of today. Black youth are looking for a word of life from their churches. In the midst of so much that causes despair, they seek a word of hope. They yearn for a faith that's worth living for. They seek to answer the call in the words of poet Mary Oliver, in *A Summer's Day*, "Tell me, what is it you plan to do with your one wild and precious life?"

Historically, the Black church has been deeply involved in tangible ways in the real lives of its people. For decades the Black church has been the center of the Black community. It has aided those in need and has been the social conscience of the nation. This concern for the social well-being of humankind is based on the acts of Jesus Christ. In the opening editorial of the *Gospel Trumpet* published in 1897, Christian Methodist Episcopal Church Bishop Lucious H. Holsey wrote, "Its purpose would be to discuss without hesitation, any phase of the civic, social, and those economic and political questions that may affect the well-being of the Church and race."[1] The Black church over these many decades has been in the business of offering life, the kind of life and hope Black youth so need. The Black church has been all about answering in the affirmative to the question, "Can these bones live?"

It is my contention that in order for these bones to continue to live, the Black church will have to pay attention to Black adolescents and do so in a variety of ways. This will require new thinking from those who are in the business of educating. First, it will require that we take seriously the call to teach and make room for those who are called to the ministry of teaching and educating our adolescents. In other words, it will be imperative that those who lead the educational ministry of the Black church have a heart for that work. Furthermore, it is my argument that the Black church will have to move from an educational ministry that relies mainly on caring volunteers to whom the church offers little equipping or education to a ministry that has a theological foundation and provides real tools for its leaders and the youth themselves. I am a strong proponent that youth ministers take advantage of programs such as graduate degree programs in youth ministry or Christian education or certificate programs that offer basic equipping in these areas. In many cases this will mean that the Black church redirects budgets to support the laity and clergy in theological education. This will aid immensely in the faith formation process of Black adolescents. If their leaders are better equipped to help them address the deep and probing questions at the heart of their faith, youth are likely to experience a greater level of connection with their faith and grow into more grounded and faithful adults. Faith formation connects Black adolescents with service and love. It is helping them to come to know what it means to love God and love neighbor. When formed in the faith, adolescents will show it by the presence of love for God and others.

Participants in our research seemed to hold some well-formed perspectives on the role of the Black church in helping its members address the violence and oppression encountered disproportionately by African Americans. During our focus groups, participants spoke emphatically and clearly when asked, "What does the Black church have to do with all of this?"

The Black Church from Adolescent Eyes

When asked about the Black church's role, participants had a variety of words. Here are just a few. I have taken this representative sample of participants' comments and put them in social, political, justice, and economics categories.

1. Poverty—explained as always needing money *Economics*

2. Nice building in the 'hood—the largest building in the neighborhood *Economics*

3. Single parent—many of the people of my church did not have husbands *Social*

4. Being a statistic—a male who has experienced the death of friends *Social*

5. Firearms, controlled substances—not inside the church but all around the church *Social/Political*

6. Trying to rescue family—a place where people in need come to see *Social*

7. Break generational cycles—this is what the church should do *Social*

8. Family—members of my family attend *Social*

9. No exposure to social issues—not taught or preached *Social*

10. Two-parent household—living in private world; sheltered until high school *Social*

11. Everything centered on Black neighborhood *Social*

12. Saw class distinctions but identified with all *Social*

13. Mentors in the past but not now *Social*

14. Having a village; lived close *Social*

15. Older generation linked to civil rights *Justice*

16. Now destruction of home, stay in place; used to be school and church *Social*

17. There is a modern-day Jim Crow—talking about incarceration of Blacks *Social/Political*

18. Now church has less presence *Social*

19. Church provided individual exposure to the world *Social*

20. Church lacking in exposing, investing; community is different but church does not change *Economics/Social*

21. Churches are not developing *Economics/Social*

22. Status held about everything *Social*
23. Institutions are top-heavy *Political*
24. There is a disconnect with generations *Social*
25. Need intergenerational knowledge *Social*
26. There is emotional trauma *Social*
27. Integration/slavery taken away; history lost; whitewashing history *Justice*

For some Black adolescents, the Black church has been a place that has spoken primarily to social issues; however, not all of the issues are related to social justice. In truth, their observations tell a powerful story by reflecting how very little real social justice they can see being addressed. This speaks to the multiple levels of the Black church, which is far from a monolith.

From the words of the focus group and the conversations attached to the words, I draw three conclusions concerning what I think is imperative for Black churches, their leaders, and the entire congregation to give their concerted attention. First, the issue of mass incarceration is of critical importance because of the effect it has on the availability of Black youth as it relates to their parents' ability to be present in their lives. The second conclusion addresses issues related to intergenerational ministry and the church's valuing of youth and young adults. Finally, this chapter will expand upon the role of pedagogy in equipping Black youth to see, appreciate, and live into their Christian vocations.

Mass Incarceration

During the 1990s, while in seminary, I worked part-time for a social agency that was located at the edge of what was called the projects. The agency focused on providing programs of engagement for teenagers. Every day I observed the movement within this housing complex. My observations caused me to wonder how any of the youth in this environment could be successful in school, for it seemed like they went through war zones prior to going to school each morning.

This is not to speak negatively of the housing arrangements but to highlight the trauma associated with growing up Black in America where drug use, gun violence, domestic violence, poverty, and a myriad of other social conditions that lead to post-traumatic stress disorder (PTSD), which is often labeled bad behavior in Black teens.

Conversations that I have had with Black teens and their parents over the last three decades reveal that many Black youths, regardless of where they live, have experienced and witnessed traumatizing events. Many have learned of traumatic events that occurred to a close family member or friend. Additionally, repeated news accounts of the details of the deaths, often complete with graphic video, also cause stress to these adolescents.

THE CASE OF BOB: Bob was a young Black man accused of a crime he says he did not commit. I served as a mentor to this young man starting when he was in the eighth grade, and I believed his story because we had a strong relationship where I had become one in whom he confided. This relationship began when I became his pastor and leader of his Enlightened Males group. Several weeks after the accusation, police came to his house and arrested him. He called me, and I did everything in my power to get him released from custody, but he had to spend the night in jail until the judge set bail at ten thousand dollars the next day. Fortunately, he had another mentor who was able to pay the thousand dollars to set him free. When he reappeared in court the judge pushed the hearing date out one month. While I was in the courthouse, a large group of men, the majority Black, had to go back to jail because they did not have anyone to post bail. I shared with Bob my disgust with this system. I wondered how many people across this country face the same fate of being in jail because they don't have bail money. It seems that we have a system that says you are guilty until you prove you are innocent; therefore, you reside in jail. It leads to the mass incarceration of many Blacks.

The stress of living in poverty often leads to many of the aforementioned traumas, which then result in adolescents dropping out of school and eventually even arrest and prison time, if not death. One of the major effects of the way America views and treats African American adolescents is mass incarceration. I highlight this specifically as a part of what the Black church must address. However, the overall issue of poverty and its subset of issues, such as psychological trauma, have to be addressed if the church is going to be serious in its ministry to Black adolescents.

I begin this argument by stating the obvious. The availability of Black adolescents should be a concern for older generations. One reason for this concern is mass incarceration. I am not claiming that Black youth are criminals—far from it! Rather, Black youth are victims of systems that unfairly and disproportionately incarcerate them. I have been to court with parishioners on numerous occasions as a pastor and observed the number of young Black men who await some judgment. There is no question in my mind: the school-to-prison pipeline was designed and honed into an efficient way to remove Black adolescents, male and female, from their communities and support systems at a time in their lives when it will have the greatest detrimental effect. Mass incarceration was designed to reinforce systemic racism and oppression. Let me offer a story to illustrate.

Research gives some reasons for mass incarceration, including

1. Exorbitant bail,
2. Mandatory minimum sentencing,
3. "Three strikes" laws,
4. "Truth in sentencing" laws,
5. The "war on drugs,"
6. Plea bargaining resulting from harsh punishment for non-violent crimes,
7. Problematic probation and parole,

8. Inadequate mental health care,

9. Longer sentences and more life sentences, and

10. The expansion of private prisons and profit motives for incarceration.[2]

The Black church of the twenty-first century, in its efforts to excel in faith formation of adolescents, must include addressing mass incarceration. It has an effect on the presence of youth in communities and in the lives of their families and children. I applaud the efforts of churches that have prison and aftercare ministries and celebrate the hope they offer by helping incarcerated people maintain connections with their families and children. However, there is so much more to be done to dismantle the system of mass incarceration in the first place. For churches this is both/and: to help those victimized by it and to work for a more just system.

Bob did not go to prison but had to obtain an attorney that he could not afford who led him to plead guilty to reduce his chances of going to prison. As a result of this charge Bob lost a job and had to find other employment where he was overqualified and required to work Sundays. In the meantime, the adolescent son that Bob is raising as a single parent is not available to attend church and engage in youth ministry. The effects and collateral consequences of incarceration must also be addressed.

Rachel Condry and Shona Mason, in "Conceptualizing the Effects of Imprisonment on Families," argue that

> the imprisonment of one person does not simply affect that person alone but can harm an entire community. Often times, men and women who are incarcerated leave behind children and struggling caregivers. Research on parental incarceration suggests that paternal and maternal incarceration tends to compromise a child's wellbeing. For instance, children of incarcerated parents tend to be at a higher risk of school dropout, physical and mental health issues,

drug use, anti-social behaviors, and increased contact
with the criminal justice system.[3]

The case of Bob shows how adolescents of parents caught up in this
unjust system of mass incarceration can also be casualties and become
church dropouts, disconnected from their best networks of support.
Whole families are negatively impacted in short- and long-term ways
by this system. It is the Black church's responsibility to offer care and
support and to work for justice.

Intergenerational Considerations

As I have listened to youth over the years, I have frequently heard
comments like this one from focus group participants: "There is a disconnect with generations." I don't claim this as unique to the Black
church or to any one generation, but it is huge when it comes to faith
formation of Black adolescents in the twenty-first century. This comment makes me wonder about the experiences of adolescents that led
them to feel this way, and it leads me to think in terms of intergenerational ministry.

Allow me to offer a story reflecting the distinction between intergenerational ministry and a group of people of various ages sharing
the same space. My local church has had a tradition of giving graduates a huge celebration. It started with two middle-aged educators of
the church who had a strong interest in the welfare of the children
and youth. These women led the congregation in celebrating the
achievements of the children and youth of each level of movement in
school. So, from kindergarten graduation all the way to college graduation and beyond, there was a party during the month of May or
June for graduates. This year I took notice of who was in attendance.
Those over sixty-five were mainly in attendance and represented
the demographic of the church. In previous years there was a larger
distribution of ages because of the different composition of the
congregation. At one time, I might have considered this to be

intergenerational ministry because of the diversity of ages. As many churches are finding, though, simple proximity doesn't equal relationships. Being in the same room does open the possibility for relationships, but it's not the whole answer to the problem of the adult-youth divide many of us experience in our congregations.

In recent years, I have come to understand intergenerational and multi-generational ministry differently. *Intergenerational* is generally understood as members of two or more different generations having some degree of mutual, influential relationship developed through cooperative interaction to achieve common goals instead of multigenerational settings, where several generations are in proximity with each other but not necessarily engaged in meaningful relationships.[4] Each Sunday in the pastor's office, I look at a picture taken almost thirty years ago of a choir. In that picture are children, youth, young adults, and senior adults. I have often referred to this as an intergenerational choir, but I cannot know the kinds of relationships present among those in the photo just by looking.

In my denomination and many others, educational ministry takes place almost exclusively through age-level ministries. Seldom, if ever, are intergenerational ministries organized or attempted. Healthy congregations foster both relationships among those of the same age group and across age groups, so why wouldn't congregations attempt intergenerational ministries more often? In short, because it is complicated and difficult to help people do something in the congregation that they don't do very well anywhere else in their lives—that is, truly relate with those of other age groups.

What are some of the ramifications if the Black church were to commit to making intergenerational ministry a reality? The young and old would learn from and care for each other. Empathy would grow. Each generation would be able to challenge one another to release their assumptions, think differently, and practice compassion. The experience would illustrate the fact that we are all teachers and learners, no matter our age. How much deeper is a faith that is rooted in the experience of those who have more and different experiences of a relationship with God? How much richer is a faith informed by the vision of a child or adolescent, full of hope and "why not" perspectives?

We Want Our Voice Heard

I heard in some focus groups the concern of adolescents about having a voice or even being seen by adults. It made me recall hearing as an adolescent my elders' voice telling us that children are to be seen and not heard. Statements like this clearly marginalize youth. Such statements, whatever their source or motive, function to put youth in their place, a place that subordinates their needs to the preferences of grown-ups. When adolescents lose their voices, they don't have a platform for sharing their hopes and needs. They become marginalized and feel distant from those grown-ups. Their willingness to invest in the church diminishes with every such incident, and eventually they will likely leave the church. Why wouldn't they? Who would stay in a place where they were devalued, at least not if they didn't have to stay? Thus, the opportunity for faith formation is lost.

The Black church is challenged by Jesus' example to value all people, not to marginalize people for any reason, not sexuality, gender, ability, ethnicity, or age. Over my years as a pastor, I have seen that it takes intentionality and effort to hear all the voices. Adolescent voices often get drowned out by adults. I recall a leader of a ministry in the church coming to me saying that a youth would not listen to her. I asked, "Will you listen to the youth?" This is a lesson I learned from my daughter when she was sixteen years old. One day she said, "Daddy, you are not listening to me." I was thrown for a loop because I had been through pastoral care classes and learned the importance of listening and was even given lessons on listening. I thought I was a good listener. The lesson I learned has been invaluable and helped me see how I had been formed in this way. I had been taught as a youth that my voice was not important. I was still working to overcome that teaching. I suspect the ministry leader of the church had also been taught what I had been taught, thus, formed to think the voices of youth are secondary to ours as adults.

Routinely, faith communities exclude youth by not hearing their voices and not valuing their insights and gifts. I think in the twenty-first century, adolescent voices are bolder, and this may cause fear in older generations who were conditioned to be silent. In no way do I believe that is the intent. My notion about this sense of boldness continues to be affirmed as I have conversations with youth and some millennials. When engaging in intergenerational ministry, the church follows Jesus' example and teaching to hear and see the marginalized. As a result, ministries transform to include those often left out—of programmatic decisions, of discernment, of offering their God-given gifts. And more people connect to that "living water" the church has to offer. God calls each gathering of Jesus followers to watch out for and especially care for those on the edges. Marginalization almost always happens thoughtlessly, so we must pay close attention to who the church includes most obviously and then stretch the boundaries.

Intergenerational ministry gives space for members of all ages to share their hopes, dreams, and visions for the church. Beyond that, intergenerational ministry opens an opportunity for more imagination and creativity, for a fresh group of people with fresh eyes and fresh vision to ask, "Why not?" When only the older generation has a voice over all others, things remain relatively the same. That group sees everything as lovely and is full of nostalgia. They become comfortable and content. This is true even though what has always been done is often not the best thing for progress and church growth. And the older generations bring gifts to an intergenerational ministry context, as well, by offering encouragement when roadblocks appear or perspective from many years of experience. Each generation's struggles are both unique and universal. As a result, commonality and difference are discovered when young, old, and all in between share their ideas together. This is wonderful for several reasons. First, each generation learns something new. Second, creativity is given life. Third, never-before-imagined events are tried. Fourth, more people in the congregation take ownership of what takes place.

The Black church must encourage all ages to share their ideas and give outlets for expression. More people will be retained when they experience their perspectives valued. More people listening for God's voice and God's call will lead to stagnant theological perspectives being challenged and ideologies examined. Though this can cause some discomfort, it also facilitates spiritual growth and humility.

If the church is comprised of a greater variety of ages, the age makeup of leaders should be considered. Those invited to serve in a leadership capacity are more often than not older adults. Each generation brings to the table a unique perspective. So, we must include a wide range of ages on governing bodies and ministry teams. Youth, even if accompanied by a parent for support, can make fantastic leaders with creative ideas. If we believe God creates all people to have unique gifts, then why wouldn't God gift some younger people with discernment, wisdom, and leadership? And why would the church not call out those gifts and invite younger people into leadership?

Youth and Young Adults in Worship

As I have mentioned in previous chapters, the Black church must pay special attention to the role of worship and music in the faith formation of adolescents. What better place for a real intergenerational ministry focus than in the context of the worship service with the opportunity to engage youth and mentor them at the same time? It is also a time of sharing perspectives concerning worship. The Black church must cultivate an attitude of seriously listening to youth, really hearing them. Youth must not be dismissed as too young and inexperienced to be able to engage fully in worship. As adults we have to help Black adolescents feel and understand they have ownership. In doing so we are helping them to participate in the co-creation work of God.

In most studies concerning intergenerational worship, the emphasis seems to be on keeping youth from leaving the church: "If we keep them involved, they will not leave the church." This is not our motivation here. I am proposing integrational worship with one focus in mind, that is, formation of faith. Why worship intergenerationally, and what does it have to do with faith formation of Black adolescents? Everyone needs to have relationships with generations beyond themselves—adolescents included. Intergenerational worship helps youth grow a sense of belonging. Corporate worship helps us understand who God is from the perspectives of others; it helps us see how others respond in faithfulness. Intergenerational worship that is truly intergenerational is a powerful context for the formation of a multidimensional and vibrant faith.

Now I turn my attention to the final conclusion I draw from the research of Black adolescents in the church. I might add these conclusions are the direction I envision for educational ministry in the twenty-first century. It is another way for the Black church to answer in the affirmative to the question, "Can these bones live?"

Pedagogy

The Black church has been an exemplar of education. The Black family has been the epitome of resiliency and adaptation. Black adolescents are ever facing challenges that go beyond our own experiences. It is my contention we must not allow complacency, apathy, and comfortability to override the needs of our youth such that we insist on familiar methods of teaching and learning. What is tried and true is often also tired and in effective. I am proposing two forms of pedagogy that lend themselves to transformation, and not only transmission of knowledge. One I discussed in Chapter 5, critical pedagogy, which I will mention only briefly here. The second is contemplative pedagogy, which I will say more about.

Critical Pedagogy

In light of the developmental place of adolescents, those who lead youth in teaching and learning contexts are called to focus on developing critical pedagogy. By critical pedagogy, I mean developing strategies to deconstruct power in formal learning settings such that teachers facilitate student discovery rather than deposit information into students as objects of learning. To participate in their education as members of a democratic process, resistance to unequal power structures must be addressed. By engaging in teaching and learning dialogically and developing the skills needed to think critically about society, youth are empowered to develop not only academically but civically and personally. A part of this personal development is faith formation.

A young adult once gave me a good example of the use of critical pedagogy. She told me about her experience in the radio business. Some Black enterprises, including the radio stations she worked for, were largely supported by payday loan services. These payday loan services charge exorbitant interest rates that feed into the harrowing debt cycle that many people, including their radio audience, experience. Critical pedagogy, seeking to name the issue, asks, "Who is determining what listeners are exposed to?" In fact, whoever has this power, although they play Black gospel music and local church sermons that intend to liberate and inspire those who face financial and other despair, has little interest in exposing the target audience to alternative financing options. Effectively, working-class people who listen to the Black gospel radio station and do business with loan sharks are further socialized into the working class rather than achieving the financial freedom or stability that they seek. An empowered learner listening to these advertisements will stop and ask those penetrating questions. Learners who "want to know what they are not being taught as well as what they are being told" would be far less likely to become lost in the consumerism that is tied to poverty.[5]

Another example of how the use of critical pedagogy could be specifically helpful in Christian education settings has to do with gambling. It is not unusual in some Black churches to teach that gambling is a sin; therefore, Christians ought not to go to casinos. At the same time, congregations engage in raffling televisions, gas, gift cards, or other prizes. Using critical pedagogy, one might be led to question whether raffles are a form of gambling. Reflection on this question by a congregation might address how one wins a raffle (by purchasing one or more tickets or chances to win). How many people have to lose for another to win? Why are raffles held in the first place? The answer to these questions could lead to identifying the real issue as stewardship, and an action might be to teach classes on stewardship so that some direction might be given on the use of money. Engaging critical pedagogy is essential in teaching and learning contexts with Black adolescents.

Contemplative Pedagogy

Contemplative pedagogy shifts the focus of teaching and learning to incorporate first-person approaches which connect learners to their lived, embodied experience of their own learning. Black adolescent learners are encouraged to become more aware of their internal world and connect their learning to their own values and sense of meaning, which in turn enables them to form richer, deeper, relationships with their peers, their communities, and the world around them.

Why should the Black church form its youth in faith through contemplative pedagogy? The Christian life is not a static one. It is moving us someplace, and the Holy Spirit is our faithful companion, faithful to guide us to the place we are to be. Ralph Waldo Emerson once said, "You are what you think all day long."[6] I wouldn't go so far as to say that we are defined by our thoughts, but two thousand years of Christian practices and tradition remind us that we become what we do. Our hearts are formed by, and our lives are shaped into, the practices we live out in our day-to-day lives. The danger in talking about spiritual practices, though, is that they can quickly slip from formative into legalistic, and then the old saying starts to ring true: "We only belong if we behave."

I'd like to pull those of us in the Black church away from a legalistic view of teaching and learning and remind us that all good things take time. As any craftsperson knows, the formation of something requires diligence and patience. We are not now what we will be one day, that's true. However, we need not always be what we are right now. From the beginning, the church has used spiritual practices to aid and spur on the spiritual life.

Let me offer two contemplative practices. One is lectio divina. It is a contemplative way of reading the Bible. This is not a Bible study but a way to teach adolescents how to allow the Scripture to speak to them as a method of faith formation and spiritual transformation. Faith formation and spiritual transformation take place as Black youth would read a Scripture and reflect upon such questions as, "How is my life touched by this reading?" or "What is my response to God as a result of reading this Scripture?"

A second practice is mindfulness. A widely circulated definition of mindfulness from Jon Kabat-Zinn is this: "Mindfulness is the awareness that arises from paying attention on purpose, in the present moment, and nonjudgmentally."[7] Mindfulness cultivates deepened awareness, concentration, and insight. Tobin Hart states, "Inviting the contemplative simply includes the natural human capacity for knowing through silence, looking inward, pondering deeply, beholding, witnessing the contents of our consciousness. . . . These approaches cultivate an inner technology of knowing." This cultivation is the aim of contemplative pedagogy, teaching that includes methods "designed to quiet and shift the habitual chatter of the mind to cultivate a capacity for deepened awareness, concentration, and insight."[8]

An example of mindfulness with Black adolescents might be to gather them in a circle and present Genesis 1:27 to them. Ask youth to think of persons they admire and discuss what makes that person have value. Youth can also be asked to be in dialogue with another youth and pay attention to what that person is saying.

Contemplative pedagogy not only provides a way of helping learners to concentrate more effectively but also incorporates ways of teaching and learning that can provide a different learning experience by opening up new ways of knowing. Because of the trauma and microaggressions Black youth have encountered, a disconnect can occur with their bodies that is unhealthy and unhelpful. Steps toward reconnecting all the parts of themselves can be achieved by moving beyond a technical, scientific training to incorporate body, mind, and spirit by allowing the space for adolescents to incorporate who they are and to understand how they are changed by what they learn. The importance of this was stated clearly by Daniel Barbezat in his discussion about how science and technology have often been applied in ways that create harm: "The consequences of our unwillingness to bring into the classroom our own students' sense of meaning and have them begin to build and exercise a sense of discernment about that meaning and the implications in the world are quite frankly horrifying."[9]

It seems to me that contemplative pedagogy has the potential to break the silence in the midst of silence. As Black adolescents come more in touch with who they are, they will speak in ways that are more uninhibited. They will begin to trust themselves and their ability to make meaning and discern connections. If we can quiet our grown-up voices for long enough, I believe this might provide an avenue for the church to hear our youth express themselves in regard to identity, purpose, vision, and vocation.

Conclusion

Can these bones live? For me, the answer is yes when we allow God to breathe the Holy Spirit into the bones. I was moved when, in a focus group of Black youth where I was an observer, one young woman said, "No disrespect, but we need a younger group asking us questions." Young people are about energy. They have bodies that want to move; they have emotions they want to express; and they have developing relationships that are incredibly interesting and important to them. Adults—especially in the faith community—are about status quo, maintaining equilibrium. Too often, they want young people to listen, behave, be still, and stop talking—all to soothe adult fears, fulfill mission statements, and support programs. This makes young people wary and anxious.[10] It is true that adolescents can cause adults to be anxious. They will not stay still. They exaggerate and mirror adult postures that make adults self-conscious and uncomfortable. Young people can be disturbingly unpredictable and frighteningly honest. One day they seem happy to conform to their parents' wishes and adult conventions; the next day it appears they are making it up as they go along.[11]

It is precisely into the fear and anxiety that the Black church, and specifically those interested in faith formation of Black adolescents, must journey daily. Social, political, economic, spiritual concerns— there is a relationship among all of these aspects of life. The Black church cannot afford to hide behind the ideology of separation of church and state. The Black church has always understood that there is no dichotomy between the secular and sacred.

By living into the heritage and legacy that is the best of the Black church, we can acknowledge the strength and vibrancy of Black adolescence and celebrate the many gifts they bring to the church. Can these dry bones live? If the church is willing to allow time for the sinews to come onto the bones, to allow the awkwardness of newly re-formed bodies to dissipate, to love that which has been and that which is yet to come, and to embrace the new life God has brought among us, even in us. Can these dry bones live? Yes, if the church allows space for adolescents—and more than that, if we acknowledge that, in God's eyes, the space is as much theirs as it is ours as elders. Yes, if the church fosters their lives intentionally by using its collective power to creating more just, equitable, and life-affirming contexts for all. Yes, if the church partners with one another, celebrating each other's gifts, for the blessing of all and the glory of God.

NOTES

1. *CME Discipline* 2018 (Memphis: CME Publishing House, 2018), 131.

2. "Mass Incarceration and Mass Punishment," Fair Fight Initiative, https://www.fairfightinitiative.org/the-history-causes-and-facts-on-mass-incarceration/.

3. Rachel Condry and Shona Mason, "Conceptualizing the Effects of Imprisonment on Families: Collateral Consequences, Secondary Punishment, or Symbiotic Harms?", January 28, 2020, Theoretical Criminology, https://journals.sagepub.com/doi/10.1177/1362480619897078.

4. Feliciano Villar, "Intergenerational or Multigenerational? A Question of Nuance," *Journal of Intergenerational Relationships* 5, no. 1 (2007): 115–17.

5. Ira Shore, *Empowering Education: Critical Teaching for Social Change* (Chicago: University of Chicago Press, 1992), 36.

6. Ralph Waldo Emerson quotes, Goodreads, https://www.goodreads.com/quotes/114540-you-become-what-you-think-about-all-day-long.

7. Steve Paulson, Richard Davidson, Amishi Jha, and Jon Kabat-Zinn, "Becoming Conscious: The Science of Mindfulness," *Annals of the New York Academy of Sciences* 1303 (2013): 87–104, https://centerhealthyminds.org/assets/files-publications/PaulsonBecomingAotNYAoS.pdf.

8. "Tobin Hart," ChildSpirit Institute, https://childspirit.org/tobin-hart-ph-d/.

9. "Contemplative Pedagogy with Daniel Barbezat," speaking at Syracuse University, October 15, 2013, https://www.youtube.com/watch?v=Y5iARQfWRZQ.

10. Ibid.

11. Ibid.

Selected Bibliography

Barna Group. "Racial Divides in Spiritual Practices." January 12, 2017. https://www.barna.com/research/racial-divides-spiritual-practice/.

Benin, M., and V. M. Keith. "The Social Support of Employed African American and Anglo Mothers." *Journal of Family Issues* 16 (1995): 275–97.

Blasingame, John W. *The Slave Community: Plantation Life in the Antebellum South*. New York: Oxford University Press, 1972.

Brittain, Aerika S. "Understanding African American Adolescents' Identity Development: A Relational Developmental Systems Perspective." *Journal of Black Psychology* 38, no. 2 (May 2012): 172–200. https://www.researchgate.net/publication/233931724_Understanding_African_American_Adolescents%27_Identity_Development_A_Relational_Developmental_Systems_Perspective.

Cabrera, N., O. Jaquette, R. Marx, and J. Milem. "Missing the (Student Achievement) Forest for All the (Political) Trees: Empiricism and the Mexican-American Studies Controversy in Tucson." *American Educational Research Journal* 51, no. 6 (2014): 1084–1118.

Cammarota, J. "A Social Justice Approach to Achievement: Guiding Latina/o Students Toward Educational Attainment with a Challenging, Socially Relevant Curriculum." *Equity & Excellence in Education* 40, no. 1 (2007): 87–96.

Carter, D. J. "Cultivating a Critical Race Consciousness for African-American School Success." *Educational Foundations* 22, no. 1-2 (2008): 11–28.

Cohen, S., L. Brittney, and B. H. Gottlieb. *Social Support Measurement and Intervention: A Guide for Health and Social Scientists*. New York: Oxford University Press, 2000.

Condry, Rachel, and Shona Mason. "Conceptualizing the Effects of Imprisonment on Families: Collateral Consequences, Secondary Punishment, or Symbiotic Harms?" January 28, 2020. Theoretical Criminology. https://journals.sagepub.com/doi/10.1177/1362480619897078.

Crutchfield, Carmichael. *The Formation of a People: Christian Education in the African American Church*. Valley Forge, PA: Judson Press, 2020.

Denton, Melinda, and Christian Smith. *Soul Searching: The Religious and Spiritual Lives of American Teenagers*. New York: Oxford University Press, 2005.

Dee, Thomas, and Emily Penner. "The Causal Effects of Cultural Relevance: Evidence from an Ethnic Studies Curriculum." CEPA Working Paper No. 16-01 (2016). Stanford Center for Education Policy Analysis. https://cepa.stanford.edu/sites/default/files/wp16-01-v201601.pdf.

Diemer, M., A. Voight, and R. Watts. "Critical Consciousness: Current Status and Future Directions." *New Directions for Child and Adolescent Development* 134 (2011): 43–57.

Diemer, M., L. Rapa, C. Park, and J. Perry. "Development and Validation of a Critical Consciousness Scale." *Youth & Society* (2014): 1–23.

English, Devin, Sharon F. Lambert, Brendisha M. Tynes, Lisa Bowleg, Maria Cecelia Zea, and Lionel C. Howard. "Daily Multidimensional Racial Discrimination among Black U.S. American Adolescents." *Journal of Applied Developmental Psychology* 66 (January–February 2020). https://doi.org/10.1016/j.appdev.2019.101068.

"The Enslaved Family." In the Making of African American Identity: volume 1, 1500–1865. National Humanities Center. Toolbox Library: Primary Resources in U.S. History and Literature, 2007. http://nationalhumanitiescenter.org/pds/maai/community/text1/text1read.htm.

Feinstein, Sheryl. *Secrets of the Teenage Brain*. Thousand Oaks, CA: Corwin, 2009.

Forde, A. T., D. M. Crookes, S. F. Suglia, and R. T. Demmer. "The Weathering Hypothesis as an Explanation for Racial Disparities in Health: A Systematic Review." *Annals of Epidemiology* 33 (2019): 1–18.e3.

Geronimus, A. T., M. Hicken, D. Keene, and J. Bound. "'Weathering' and Age Patterns of Allostatic Load Scores among Blacks and Whites in the United States." *American Journal of Public Health* 96, no. 5 (2016): 826–33.

Ginwright, Shawn. *Black Youth Rising: Activism and Racial Healing in Urban America*. New York: Teachers College Press, 2010.

Gunnoe, Marjorie Lindner, and Claudia DeVries Beversluis. "Youth, Worship, and Faith Formation: Findings from a National Survey." Reformed Worship. https://www.reformedworship.org/article/march-2009/youth-worship-and-faith-formation.

Hamilton, S. F. "An Ecological Approach to Adolescent Development and School." *Human Ecology Forum* 12 (1982): 2–6.

Huyser-Honig, Joan, and James Abbington. "African American Church Music: Beyond the Myths." May 14, 2014. Calvin Institute of Christian Worship. https://worship.calvin.edu/resources/resource-library/african-american-church-music-beyond-the-myths.

Janssen, Denise. *Fostering Faith: Teaching and Learning in the Christian Church*. Valley Forge, PA: Judson Press, 2014.

———, ed. *Educating for Redemptive Community: Essays in Honor of Jack Seymour and Margaret Ann Crain*. Eugene, OR: Wipf & Stock, 2015.

Keeley, Robert, ed. *Shaped by God: Twelve Essentials for Nurturing Faith in Children, Youth, and Adults*. Grand Rapids, MI: Faith Alive Christian Resources, 2010.

Kohlberg, Lawrence. "Moral Development and the Education of Adolescents." In *Adolescents and the American High School*, edited by R. F. Purnell. New York: Holt, Rinehart, and Winston, 1970.

Krause, N., and E. Bastida. "Church-based Social Relationships, Belonging, and Health among Older Mexican Americans." *Journal for the Scientific Study of Religion* 50, no. 2 (January 2011): 397–409.

Lincoln. C. Eric, and Lawrence H. Mamiya. *The Black Church in the African American Experience*. Durham, NC: Duke University Press, 1990.

Mattis, J. S. "African American Women's Definitions of Spirituality and Religiosity." *Journal of Black Psychology* 26, no. 1 (2000): 101–22.

McAdoo, Harriet. "Interpreting the Afro-American Heritage in the Afro-American Family Organization." In *Black Families*, edited by Niara Suderkass. Thousand Oaks, CA: Sage, 1981.

McEwen, B. S. "Protective and Damaging Effects of Stress Mediators." *New England Journal of Medicine* 338, no. 3 (1998): 171–79.

McMickle, Marvin A. *An Encyclopedia of African American Christian Heritage*. Valley Forge, PA: Judson Press, 2002.

Mitchell, Henry H. *Black Belief: Folk Beliefs of Blacks in America and West Africa*. New York: Harper and Row, 1975.

Moffitt, Ursula, Linda P. Juang, and Moin Syed. "Intersectionality and Youth Identity Development in Europe." *Psychology* 31 (January 2020). Frontiers in Psychology. https://www.frontier sin.org/articles/10.3389/fpsyg.2020.00078/full.

National Urban League. *The State of Black America: Portrait of the Black Male*. Silver Spring, MD: Beckham's Group, 2007.

O'Connor, C. "Dispositions Toward Collective Struggle and Educational Resilience in the Inner City: A Case Analysis of Six

African-American High School Students." *American Educational Research Journal* 34, no. 4 (1997): 593–629.

Parker, Evelyn L. *Trouble Don't Last Always: Emancipatory Hope for African American Adolescents*. Cleveland: Pilgrim Press, 2003.

Raboteau, Albert J. *Slave Religion: The "Invisible Institution" in the Antebellum South*. New York: Oxford University Press, 1978.

Rogers, J., and V. Terriquez. *Learning to Lead: The Impact of Youth Organizing on the Educational and Civic Trajectories of Low-Income Youth*. Los Angeles: Institute for Democracy, Education, and Access, 2013.

Sanders, M. G. "Overcoming Obstacles: Academic Achievement as a Response to Racism and Discrimination." *Journal of Negro Education* 66, no. 1 (1997): 83–93.

Schnase, Robert, *Five Practices of a Fruitful Congregation*. Nashville: Abingdon, 2018.

Shore, Ira. *Empowering Education: Critical Teaching for Social Change*. Chicago: University of Chicago Press, 1992.

Smith, Wallace C. *The Church in the Life of the Black Family*. Valley Forge, PA: Judson Press, 1990.

Tatum, B. D. *Why Are All the Black Kids Sitting Together in the Cafeteria? And Other Conversations about Race*. New York: Basic Books, 1997.

Taylor, R. J., D. H. Chae, K. D. Lincoln, and L. M. Chatters. "Extended Family and Friendship Support Networks Are Both Protective and Risk Factors for Major Depressive Disorder, and Depressive Symptoms among African Americans and Black Caribbeans." *Journal of Nervous and Mental Disease* 203 (2015): 132–40.

Taylor, R. J., L. M. Chatters, and J. Levin. *Religion in the Lives of African Americans: Social, Psychological, and Health Perspectives*. Thousand Oaks, CA: Sage, 2004.

Trent, Maria, Danielle C. Dooley, and Jacqueline Dougé. "The Impact of Racism on Child and Adolescent Health." *Pediatrics* 148, no. 2 (August 2019). https://pediatrics.aappublications.org/content/144/2/e20191765.

Turner, Roger D. In *Black on Black Violence: Moving Towards Realistic Explanations and Solutions in Black on Black Crime*, edited by P. Ray Kedia. Bristol, IN: Wyndham Hall Press, 1994.

Vellema, Sharon. "Teens, Worship, and Faith Formation." September 10, 2013. Calvin Institute of Christian Worship. https://worship.calvin.edu/resources/resource-library/teens-worship-and-faith-formation/.

Verbanas, Patti. "Black Teens Face Racial Discrimination Multiple Times Daily, Suffer Depressive Symptoms as a Result." December 16, 2019. Medical Express. https://medicalxpress.com/news/2019-12-Black-teens-racial-discrimination-multiple.html/.

Villar, F. "Intergenerational or Multigenerational? A Question of Nuance." *Journal of Intergenerational Relationships* 5, no. 1 (2007): 115–17.

Westerhoff, John H., III. *Will Our Children Have Faith?* New York: Seabury, 1976.

Wimberly, Anne E. Streaty. "Worship in the Lives of Black Adolescents: Builder of Resilience and Hope." *Liturgy* 29, no. 1 (2014): 23–33. https://www.tandfonline.com/doi/abs/10.1080/0458063X.2014.846742.

"Youth in the Civil Rights Movement." Civil Rights History Project. Library of Congress. https://www.loc.gov/collections/civil-rights-history-project/articles-and-essays/youth-in-the-civil-rights-movement/.